THE PATIENT harnesses the power of multiple stories about Ugandans and their broken health system to deliver a powerful message on the urgent need for reform. The author's long career on the front lines of health and health policy gives her insight and experience. Her strident voice bears eloquent witness to the travails of fellow Ugandans suffering and dying due to an unaccountable and errant health system. This is a call to action that will leave few readers unmoved. *David Bishai, MD,MPH, PhD. Professor, Johns Hopkins Bloomberg School of Public Health, President International Health Economics Association*

Weaving together the story of three childhood friends, and their experiences of Mulago Hospital, Dr. Kobusingye provides an inside account of the joys and frustrations resulting from the choices made by those in positions of authority in Uganda's health sector. Their choices affect medical practitioners and patients differently. This is a book that policy makers and public interest law practitioners should read and reflect upon. *Dr. Phiona Muhwezi Mpanga, lawyer & academic, Makerere University School of Law.*

Dr. Kobusingye has cleverly combined the daily experiences of the patient and conversations between medical personnel to illustrate the painful decline of the health services in Uganda to make the statistics a reality. *Dr. Sarah Hodges, Head of Anesthesia, CoRSU Rehabilitation Hospital, Entebbe Rd, Uganda.*

THE PATIENT

SACRIFICE, GENIUS, AND GREED IN UGANDA'S HEALTHCARE SYSTEM

OLIVE KOBUSINGYE

authorHOUSE

AuthorHouse™ UK
1663 Liberty Drive
Bloomington, IN 47403 USA
www.authorhouse.co.uk
Phone: 0800 047 8203 (Domestic TFN)
+44 1908 723714 (International)

© 2019 Olive Kobusingye. All rights reserved.

No part of this book may be reproduced, stored in a retrieval system, or transmitted by any means without the written permission of the author.

Published by AuthorHouse 12/06/2019

ISBN: 978-1-7283-9585-2 (sc)
ISBN: 978-1-7283-9584-5 (e)

Print information available on the last page.

Cover photograph: Patients and their attendants wait outside a ward in New Mulago Hospital, 2012. Monitor Publications Limited.

This book is printed on acid-free paper.

Because of the dynamic nature of the Internet, any web addresses or links contained in this book may have changed since publication and may no longer be valid. The views expressed in this work are solely those of the author and do not necessarily reflect the views of the publisher, and the publisher hereby disclaims any responsibility for them.

To the women and men who taught us, not just Medicine, but how to be doctors, and how to be patient in the face of much adversity.

ACKNOWLEDGEMENTS

I am very grateful to everyone I interviewed for this book. Thank you for your generosity, and for entrusting me with your stories, some probably told for the first time ever. I hope I have told your stories well. Prof. Francis Omaswa was resourceful with contacts and reference materials. Dr. Alison Kinengyere and staff of Albert Cook Library spared no effort in locating reference materials and photographs, some a century old. I thank my friends and colleagues who encouraged me to keep writing. In particular, Drs. Maria Nsereko and Drew Ddembe gave me very helpful input into the manuscript. Dr. Patricia Spittal read every word, and her incisive comments ensured a more coherent narration. Daniel Kalinaki, in his characteristic backhanded manner, assured me that the story was worth telling. David Sseppuuya gave invaluable advice with regard to content organization, and edited the entire manuscript. My husband and our daughters were exceedingly patient with me – seemingly never doubting that the book would one day be done. Thank you so very much, everyone!

CONTENTS

How was this book compiled? xi

How did we get here? 1
The Sweet & Sour Sixties 17
The Scary Seventies 27
The Enigmatic Eighties 38
The Nutty Nineties 60
The Mucky Millennium 81
The Tottering Teens 147

Makerere University anthem (abridged) 215

HOW WAS THIS BOOK COMPILED?

In addition to desk research, the author conducted extensive interviews with many of the people who feature in this book. She personally interviewed the persons listed below, and the quotes and accounts attributed to them are drawn directly from those conversations. Unattributed opinions and conclusions are entirely those of the author.

Dr. Adam Kimala, general surgeon. Kimala worked at Mulago Hospital for most of his career until he retired from public service in 2005. By late 2019, he was working part time at Kampala Hospital.

Dr. Anthony Gakwaya, general surgeon. Gakwaya worked at Mulago Hospital as a surgeon until his retirement from public service. Dean, School of Medicine, St. Augustine International University, Uganda.

Dr. Byarugaba Baterana, physician, Director, Mulago National Referral Hospital (2011 -)

Dr. Francis Mutyaba, orthopedic surgeon. Mutyaba graduated as a doctor in 1979, and completed his general surgical training in 1984. He worked at Mulago as a surgeon for twenty years until his retirement in 2004. He continues to teach on the Makerere post-graduate program as an Honorary Lecturer.

Dr. Henry Ddungu, physician and hemato-oncologist, the Uganda Cancer Institute.

Dr. Jackie Mabweijano, Accident & Emergency surgeon. She graduated as a surgeon in 1998, and other than periods of additional training outside Uganda, she continues to work as a surgeon at Mulago Hospital.

Dr. Robert Wangoda, general surgeon. Wangoda graduated from Makerere as a doctor in 1995 and as a surgeon in 2001. He worked in Gulu and Mulago hospitals, before moving to Masaka Regional Hospital in 2013. He heads the Surgical Department.

Prof. Charles Olweny, oncologist, first Ugandan Head of the Uganda Cancer Institute, and Chair of the Board of Directors, Uganda Cancer Institute (2019 -).

Prof. Francis Omaswa, cardiothoracic surgeon. Former Director General of Health Services, Ministry of Health, former Chair of the Board of Directors, Mulago Hospital. Executive Director, African Center for Global Health & Social Transformation (ACHEST)

Dr. Jackson Orem, oncologist. Director, Uganda Cancer Institute.

Prof. Moses Galukande, general surgeon. Head, Department of Surgery, Makerere University.

Prof. Nelson Sewankambo, physician, epidemiologist. Former Dean of Makerere Medical School, and the first Principal of the College of Health Sciences.

Prof. Paul D'Arbela, cardiologist, first Ugandan cardiologist. Former Head of Department of Medicine, Makerere Medical School.

Prof. Charles Ibingira, surgeon, Principal, College of Health Services (2015 -)

Prof. Bwogi Richard Kanyerezi, physician. Former Head of Department of Medicine, Makerere Medical School. Consultant, Kampala Hospital.

Prof. Sarah Kiguli, pediatrician, medical education specialist. Former Head of Department of Pediatrics, former Coordinator, Problem Based Learning, Makerere University College of Health Sciences.

Prof. Steven Kijjambu, plastic surgeon, medical education specialist. Former Head of Department of Surgery, former Dean, School of Medicine, Makerere University College of Health Sciences.

Prof. Sam Luboga, surgeon, anatomist, medical education specialist. Former Head, Department of Anatomy, Former Associate Dean (Education & Training), College of Health Sciences.

Dr. Henry Mwebesa, Director, Health Services Planning & Development, Ministry of Health (2015 -)

Ms. Josephine Nabulime, Accident & Emergency, Critical Care nurse

Conversations from PG rooms[1] are not recounts of actual conversations. They do reflect sentiments of actual doctors, and they discuss actual events and real patient encounters. The text is indented and appears in a different typeface from the main text, to distinguish it from the rest. Where facts about specific contexts are important in understanding the conversations, those facts are presented in text boxes, and references are provided. Historical sources have been used to reconstruct conversations in some instances, and the sources have been cited wherever the case arises. In a few instances, the actual names of patients have been replaced to protect their privacy.

Currencies: All conversions and historical comparisons have been derived using https://fxtop.com/en/historical-currency-converter.php, FXTOP 11 rue Kléber, 78500 Sartrouville, France.

---

[1] Postgraduate students' rooms. Every major specialty at Mulago has a room for graduate students undergoing specialist training. In Uganda such students are already licensed doctors, and they are also called Senior House Officers, to distinguish them from interns, also called Junior House Officers.

HOW DID WE GET HERE?

Medicine is a social science and politics is nothing else but medicine on a large scale.' Rudolf Karl Ludwig Virchow, nineteenth-century German physician (1821-1902)

In 2015 the United Nations Children's Fund (UNICEF) and Uganda's Ministry for Gender, Labour, and Social Affairs released a very disturbing report about the state of Uganda's children. The 190-page document was summarized thus:

> 'Uganda is among the top 10 countries for high maternal, newborn and child mortality. HIV/AIDS is the second leading cause of death among adolescents. Malaria, diarrhoea, pneumonia and infections like HIV account for more than 70% of under-five deaths. Although basic health care is officially free, families meet 61% of their children's health care costs. There is a lack of trained health workers, health centres frequently run out of drugs and only 58% of births are attended by a skilled provider. High levels of stunting (33%), iodine deficiency and babies born with a low birth weight cause the country to lose US$899 million worth of productivity every year. More than half of Uganda's children are living in poverty. This does not just mean that their households have a low income, it includes being deprived of the things that enable children to thrive – food, shelter, clean water, sanitation, education and information. Nearly one-third of children do not have access to safe water.'[2]

---

[2] Extract from 'Situation analysis of children in Uganda 2015. Ministry of Gender, Labour and Social Development and UNICEF Uganda, 2015.' (https://www.unicef.org/uganda/media/1791/file) accessed on 13 July 2019.

Every parent, and every Ugandan concerned for the country's future should have sat up and paid attention. But in 2015 Uganda was at the height of a major political convulsion in preparation for the 2016 general elections. It is doubtful that the average voter would have come across the report. In the aftermath of the election the politicking did not stop. It was time for the ruling party to reward the enablers of the heavily contested victory, and for the opposition to regroup and continue on the well-trodden path of civil protest in the face of continuing eroding freedoms and a government that lived beyond its means, with impunity. The economy was in crisis, most government departments were running on shoestring budgets, and it would seem that not enough attention was paid to the looming crisis of Ugandan children and their struggle for survival.

In 2018 the World Bank put out a report that got a little more traction. It was as red a flag as an organization such as the Bank could wave, with damning revelations and somber language. The state of Ugandan children was very worrying indeed. After an elaborate description of the great odds stacked up against children in Uganda, and the dismal outcomes that follow such odds, the summary statement read thus:

> 'Uganda is one of the countries at the bottom of the Human Capital Index (HCI), and she is failing to provide millions of children with basic things such as a proper diet, education, and healthcare in their formative years ... 29 out of 100 are stunted and so at risk of cognitive and physical limitations that can last a lifetime. ... As a result, a child born in Uganda in 2018 will only achieve 38 per cent of his/her productive potential in life because of the limited investments [particularly in health and education] that the country makes in developing children.'[3]

For a country whose political leadership did not spend a day without talking about how close Uganda was from attaining 'middle-income

---

[3] World Bank. 2019. Human Capital Index, from World Development Report 2019: The Changing Nature of Work. Washington, DC: World Bank. doi:10.1596/978-1-4648-1328-3. License: Creative Commons Attribution CC BY 3.0 IGO

status', this was grim news. In reality though, it was news only to the elite and economically comfortable. The average low-income Ugandan was well acquainted with the conditions that the report described. They knew that their children were going to bed hungry and not learning much. They did not need reminding that the scrawny children fetching water from muddy streams, and waving cheerfully at the expensive cars that plied the roads, would be better off if they ate more, and if there were medicines at health centers when they were sick. They were well aware that too many of them died well before their time – they buried them. The women knew all about the joy of expecting a baby, the dread of labor with little medical assistance, and for some, the harrowing sense of loss at or soon after birth. So the World Bank Report was mostly discussed by those that were somewhat removed from the vulnerabilities described.

To be fair, there were already many attempts to try and get the health of Ugandans in better shape. The primary school curriculum required children as young as seven to memorize the list of the six childhood killer diseases. The children might be malnourished, some might not be fully immunized, but they needed to know about diphtheria and whooping cough. The Ministry of Health was well into the third year of their five-year strategic and investment plan, on top of which were added priorities that had not been foreseen in the plans, such as the construction of a private, highly specialized hospital. Various other ministries with mandates concerning the health and wellbeing of children – such as education; gender, labor, and social development; and agriculture, also had impressive plans. They were also hopelessly underfunded. It was against this backdrop that Uganda's relationship with FINASI, an Italian company with business interests in a number of African countries, was born.

***

When the International Specialized Hospital of Uganda (ISHU) at Lubowa, Wakiso District opens, it will have no problem attracting clients. It became a household name before the foundation was dug, and its architectural drawings became a virtual icon for modern health care. It owes its fame – or notoriety – to the fascinating story of its creation.

Once upon a time (probably February 2013) an Italian investor picked interest in the wellbeing of Ugandans, and traveled to Uganda with plans to build a modern hospital. She was well received. A Good Samaritan must have quickly conveyed her to State House, but not before, as she complained to the President, an official at the Ministry of Health tried to frustrate her noble intentions by soliciting a bribe. The official was summarily dismissed. Ms. Enrica Pinetti's good intentions met with great enthusiasm, and the rest could have been history. But that would have been a boring Ugandan story. The rest was, in fact, high drama.

Pinetti's company, FINASI, got together with a local firm, ROKO Construction LTD, to form a new entity, FINASI/ROKO Construction SPV Ltd, for the express purpose of designing, building, equipping, and staffing the Lubowa hospital. In 2014, the President laid a foundation stone for the hospital on a piece of land that had previously been a part of Joint Clinical Research Center (JCRC), but that was embroiled in controversy. A family linked to the Buganda Royals claimed that the government had grabbed their land, and a legal suit was in the works.

Between November 2014 and December 2018, a series of legally-binding agreements were made between the Government of Uganda represented by the Ministry of Finance, and FINASI/ROKO. This was a Public-Private Partnership (PPP). The sum total of these agreements was that FINASI/ROKO would indeed build, equip and staff the hospital, and that Uganda would pay for it over a period of six years, beginning two years after commencement of the construction. Uganda was to pay a tidy sum of US$ 379.7 million (1.4 trillion Uganda shillings) for the hospital. FINASI/ROKO was to source for the funding, and Promissory Notes for this amount were to be issued by government. In this entire time, Ministry of Finance officials never once walked across the road, a stone's throw away, to ask Parliament if this was all right. And the Partnership never so much as made courtesy calls on the Ugandan medical fraternity, situated principally in a one-mile radius, in particular the professional associations, whose membership had considerable knowledge and experience concerning specialized health care. Most specialist doctors in government employment had their eyes fixed on New Mulago Hospital, which had been closed for renovation. Their patience was wearing thin as the reopening got repeatedly delayed, amidst rumors of insufficient funds. Many senior doctors therefore paid scant attention to the developments in Lubowa. They were jolted to full alert when the progress in Lubowa hit its first serious snag.

On 20 December 2018 the first Promissory Note was due, following FINASI/ROKO's presentation of the first Milestone Completion Certificate. According to the agreements, Government was obliged to hand over the Promissory Note within two days. The following day the Attorney General told the Ministry of Finance that they could not issue Promissory Notes without Parliamentary authorization. The law stipulated that 'Government shall not enter into a transaction that binds Government to a financial commitment for more than one year except where the financial commitment is authorized by Parliament.' This was not a new law. It was puzzling that the Partnership had negotiated so many financial arrangements and signed so many agreements, involving a sum that was 80% of the Ministry of Health's 2017/18 budget[4], without seeking this approval.

There was no time for finger pointing – if someone had been sleeping on the job, they had slept long enough. Ministry of Finance did not exactly run across the road to ask Parliament for help, but in February 2019, they did the next best thing. They presented Parliament with a brief: 'On the Proposal to issue Promissory Notes not exceeding US$ 379.71 million to FINASI/ROKO Construction SPV Ltd for the financing of the design, construction, and equipping of the International Specialized Hospital of Uganda at Lubowa.' In summary, Finance told Parliament that they had defaulted on legally-binding agreements, and that if Parliament did not hurry up with the approval, they ran the risk of having the agreements terminated. 'The termination of Project Agreements will

---

[4] Ministerial Policy Statement of the Ministry of Health for the financial year 2017/18. Ministry of Health, Kampala.

potentially lead to loss of Government monies and cause serious damage to Uganda's reputation among international investors and the international financial community.' They concluded with a simple enough request: '...authorize government, by passing a Resolution of Parliament, to issue Promissory Notes of up to US$ 379.71 million, subject to the certification of the completion of Project activities by the Ministry of Health Owner's Engineer, in line with the Bills of Exchange Act 1933.' To avoid time lost in the drafting, the Ministry of Finance attached a draft Resolution for the Clerk to Parliament to append his signature.

Parliament could have quickly obliged. A messenger could have darted across the road with the signed copy of the resolution in hand, and the Ugandan family honor would have been redeemed. But as is bound to happen when time is truly of the essence, a few people started to pick at the brief. The figure of US$ 379.71 million seemed somewhat high, even for a super-specialized hospital. Maybe they recalled that the newly opened specialized Women and Neonatal Hospital had cost a small fraction of the amount, although it had almost twice as many beds. Before long what should have been a quick remedial procedure, maybe sidestepping the usual parliamentary deliberation, now blew up into a full scale national debate on the Lubowa hospital – its worth, its true cost, and its ownership. In a sharply divided house where the opposition voice holds little sway, there were surprisingly many dissenting voices among the ruling party MPs. The Uganda Medical Association executive weighed in on the matter.[5] They pointed out that the Mulago upgrade had stalled for lack of a tiny fraction of the money now being availed to this new venture, while existing specialized facilities such as the Uganda Heart Institute and the Cancer Institute were starved of funding. The problem was not too many fine hospitals – indeed, even with this addition, Uganda would still be woefully short of quality hospital facilities. The devil, as always, was lurking in the details. The brief to Parliament contained a phrase that was worrisome to Mulago: 'Government will appropriate under the Ministry of Health

---

[5] Justus Lyatuu & Aaron Gad Orena. Doctors opposed to Lubowa hospital project. *The Observer.* 19 March 2019

Development budget *all the current expenditures on the medical treatment abroad as the major source of repayment to meet the Project Costs incurred by the Developer.*' If that happened, Mulago would continue to face hard times. Addressing the press on the Medical Association's petition to Parliament, Association president Dr. Ekwaro Obuku pointed out that for the country's transformation, the political class needed to have faith in Ugandan institutions and Ugandan professionals. Frank Asiimwe, a surgeon at Mulago, famously likened the government to a polygamous husband that neglects his old faithful wife on acquiring a new bride.

The Secretary to the Treasury, Keith Muhakanizi, was at pains to explain to the uninformed public that all was in order, and that Promissory Notes were a perfectly normal form of financing. More questions arose. At 264 beds for US$ 379 million, the ISHU was set to have the most expensive hospital beds on the continent – a million dollars per bed - and it would rival hospitals like the Mayo Clinic in USA. With Uganda's GDP among the lowest in the world, how was the cost ever going to be recouped? Why would medical tourists come to this untested institution, instead of going to South Africa or India, where tried and tested services cost less? The clock was ticking as the debate raged on. When all progress seemed doomed, the matter was escalated back to where it started – to State House. The President was quick to respond.

On 25 February 2019 President Museveni wrote to the Speaker of Parliament concerning the Lubowa hospital. His endorsement of the Lubowa project was unequivocal, and read in part:

'The Ministry of Health should assist Ms Enrica Pinetti to build her hospital at Lubowa so that referrals abroad stop and we stop the hemorrhage of an estimated $150 million per year that goes into "medical tourism" to India. The heart, the kidneys, the brain and the cancers should all be treated here."

Olive Kobusingye

TEL: 231900
FAX: 235462
EMAIL: she@statehouse.go.ug
PO/12
IN ANY CORRESPONDENCE ON
THIS SUBJECT PLEASE QUOTE NO. ....

THE REPUBLIC OF UGANDA

State House,
P. O. Box 25497,
Kampala,
Uganda.

25th February, 2019

Rt. Hon. Rebecca Kadaga
Speaker
The Parliament of Uganda
KAMPALA

INTERNATIONAL SPECIALIZED HOSPITAL OF UGANDA (ISHU) AT LUBOWA

I have been made to understand that the Parliamentary Committee on the National Economy requires my position with respect to the proposed International Specialized Hospital of Uganda (ISHU).

As I have stated at numerous occasions, including at the launch of the Hospital Project in June 2017, the Hospital Project proposed by FINASI and its Chairman Enrica Pinetti is very important in the development of Uganda in the following ways:

First, Uganda has been hemorrhaging foreign exchange by sending persons for treatment abroad at a cost of US$ 73 million per year. This figure was given to me by the Ministry of Health in 2014 and could be much higher now. I have led the fight to reverse this donation of resources from Uganda, which fight Maama Pinetti is a useful ally.

Secondly, the Hospital will create the national and regional world-class capacity to treat specialized cases such as organ and bone marrow transplant. This is a major development as very few hospitals in Sub-Saharan Africa (excluding South Africa) actually have. The international world-class capacity hospital that will be built at Lubowa will not only benefit Uganda, but also other neighboring countries, given the near proximity of the Hospital.

Thirdly, it will open Uganda's door to medical tourism and this translates into foreign exchange inflows.

The fourth benefit that the Hospital provides is creation and retention of specialized human resource. While Uganda has trained several health professionals over the years, they have left the country for many reasons including work conditions. Most doctors leave the country because there are no specialized hospitals where they can practice their specialties. Since the hospital will be here and accessible, they will be able to work and Ugandans will benefit from them.

I, therefore, wish to confirm my unquestionable support for the International Specialized Hospital of Uganda (ISHU) and request Parliament to expedite its consideration of the Project and accordingly, approve its financing arrangements, if they are in line with the law.

Yoweri K. Museveni
PRÉSIDENT

Copy to: Rt. Hon. Prime Minister
Hon. Minister of Finance, Planning and Economic Development

President Museveni's letter to the Speaker of Parliament concerning the proposed International Specialised Hospital of Uganda (ISHU) at Lubowa.

With that firm and clear guidance, the Lubowa question was settled. That should have been the end of the saga. It was not.

Barely a month after Parliament authorized the financing, it emerged that a part of the money for the construction – US$37 million - had gone missing. The Speaker of Parliament immediately called for an inquiry. Before the investigation got underway FINASI turned up at the construction site with armed men in military and police uniforms, and in the company of some Chinese, and they ordered partner ROKO's workers off the site. FINASI's Pinetti said she wished to replace ROKO with another construction company, China Power. ROKO appeared unprepared for the move, and their Chief Executive Officer was quoted as saying that the development was absurd. They were soon in court to defend their interests in the turbulent Public-Private Partnership. The 'worked-together-happily-ever-after' scenario appeared unlikely.

***

FINASI's entry onto the Ugandan health care scene may have been dramatic, but it was only one in a long line of such ventures. In October 1896 a small band of twelve medical missionaries from the Church Missionary Society in England landed at Mombasa after months at sea. Dr. Albert Ruskin Cook, the team leader, would later be knighted to become Sir Albert Cook, and the lead nurse, Katherine Timpson, would become Mrs. Cook, then Lady Cook, and champion of modern nursing and midwifery in Uganda. The missionaries traveled with a sizable quantity of medical and household supplies. They were destined for Buganda, and would be providing medical care primarily to the agents of the English monarchy, and by extension to the inhabitants of the vast territory that the Crown sought to colonize and control. If the journey thus far had been long, they were about to embark on their most challenging segment yet, a march into the interior to distant Buganda. It would take some two hundred porters and close to five months to arrive in Buganda. Cook and his party wasted no time in setting up facilities for their medical work. By May of the same year they had set up a hospital, and they then spent most of their time either treating patients, or teaching their assistants the art of caring for sick people.

By the time the First World War got underway in 1914, Mengo Hospital was already well established, and Cook and his staff were kept busy since it was one of the base hospitals. This made the need to train local medical staff urgent. In addition, there was constant demand for maternity and other medical services. The Cooks' determined effort to teach medicine and midwifery to the local people was the beginnings of formal medical training in Uganda and the region. They would soon be joined by many other doctors, both in teaching and providing medical care. While Mengo was the better established and equipped hospital initially, over time the investments at Mulago increased, especially with its role as a teaching hospital for Makerere College. By 1934 when Cook retired, the Makerere Medical School was well established and some 24 Senior African Medical Assistants had already graduated.

Panoramic view of Mulago Hospital 1931. *Albert Cook Library, College of Health Sciences, Makerere University*

Mulago Hospital Outpatient Department, 1932. In the background on the hill to the right is Makerere University College (currently Main Building, Makerere University). *Albert Cook Library, College of Health Sciences, Makerere University*

The Patient

One of the early groups of Mulago medical trainees with the Medical School principal and faculty, 1931 -1935. Back row L-R: A. Mowat, S,W. Kalibbala, J.P. Mitchell (Medical Superintendent of Mulago, and Principal of the Medical School), G.K. Makoro, A.W. Williams. Seated, L-R: S.B. Kyewalyanga, G.N. Bogere, P.B.S. Muganwa, I.S. Kadama.
Albert Cook Library, College of Health Sciences, Makerere University

Medical School class 1945 standing L-R: Raird, Muwazi, Williams, Onya, Makoro, Hutton. Seated L-R: T.T. Musisi, Latimar Musoke, Bbosa, Sewali, Lulume, Pande. *Albert Cook Library, College of Health Sciences, Makerere University*

***

In June 1945 a committee set up by the Colonial Office in London, known as the Asquith Commission, tabled their report regarding medical training in Uganda. The report recommended that a 1,000 bed hospital be built in Kampala to 'serve the people of Kampala and its environs', and to act as the teaching hospital for Makerere Medical School. Because of the huge demand on development resources following the destruction caused by the World War, the construction was deferred, although a grant had already been announced under the Colonial Development and Welfare Act. Construction plans did not resume until 1958, when all the required resources were martialed. On 23 February 1960, Governor Frederick Crawford laid the foundation stone, and the construction started in earnest. By this time the Old Mulago Hospital facilities were so outstripped by the sheer numbers of patients that some admitted patients were sleeping on the verandas. This was phenomenal growth for a facility that started as a Venereal Disease Hospital in 1913, dealing with gonorrhea and syphilis which were rampant at the time, and only converted to a general hospital in 1923. The New Mulago Hospital was opened in October 1962.

> It was late August, 2000. Karungi swung her bag over the shoulder and looked around the room one more time. The bag contained items that had been her faithful companions the last few years. A clinical coat, a well-used stethoscope, patella hammer, a coffee mug from a conference a few years back, and a digital pointer for use in presentations. On second thoughts, she took the pointer out and placed it on the table next to the room key. One always inherited stuff from PG room[6] alumni. Best to leave that for someone else. She opened the door, stood for a short while in the entrance to get accustomed to the darkness outside, and then she closed the door firmly behind her. It felt like leaving home. Karungi walked past the building that once housed the physiology lab, and that was now home to the newly created School of Biomedical Sciences. On the upper side of the uneven dirt path was a couple of old buildings – the smaller of the two had been an animal house back in the days when live animals were used in research at the medical school. The last batch of guinea pigs was eaten during the Idi Amin war in 1979, and the monkeys were set free for lack of food. Few people remembered that there was once a hippo in a special hippo pool right in front of the lab. The house now served as offices for the Department of Community Medicine. The bigger building housed the Department of Anatomy, with the famous cadaver room on the second floor, as well as histology labs and a lecture theatre. Across the parking lot on the far end was the Albert Cook Library. Karungi walked

---

[6] Postgraduate students' room. Every major specialty has a room for graduate students undergoing specialist training. In Uganda such students are already licensed doctors, and they are also called Senior House Officers, to distinguish them from interns, also called Junior House Officers.

through the poorly lit parking lot down to the road that divided Mulago Hospital from the medical school, leaving the Department of Physiology to the right and Davies Lecture Theatre to the left. At the security booth that stood guard to the hospital's administration block, she took the winding road that gave the most direct access to the Accident & Emergency Department on Level 3 of Mulago National Referral Hospital. To the right of the security booth was a rail that ran along the lower edge of the road dividing the medical school from the hospital. The rail was a key fixture in the life of medical students. Generations of students and doctors studying and working in Mulago had paid scant attention to the distinction between Mulago Hospital and Makerere Medical School, treating the institutions as one and the same. But lately there had been talk of separating the decades-old Siamese twins. The surgeons were already lining up the scalpels.

***

Dr. Emmanuel Lumu, Minister of Health, welcomes President Sir Edward Mutesa to the opening of Mulago Hospital, 16 October 1962. Extreme left is Her Royal Highness the Duchess of Kent. DS Archives

THE SWEET & SOUR SIXTIES

'Makerere, Makerere, We build for the future, The Great Makerere
Great, Great and Mighty, The walls around thee
Great, Great and Mighty,
The gates beside thee.

One day he was an ordinary physician at Mulago Hospital, teaching medical students and seeing an endless stream of patients, the next he was a cabinet minister with all the trappings that came with the title. Dr. Emmanuel Lumu, appointed the first Ugandan Minister of Health at Independence in 1962, felt like he was wearing someone else's skin. Not that he was unaccustomed to high society. He had his friend Kabaka Edward Mutesa to thank for that privilege. The attention he got as a minister though, was different. Some days he missed his more modest position at the hospital. As a minister, he had to worry, not about the patients under his care, but about the entire country's health system with all its warts and pimples. There were too many patients for too few hospitals and health workers, the medical school was largely dependent on expatriate staff, Kenya and Tanzania were unhappy that Makerere was not producing enough medical graduates for the whole region, and were threatening to start their own schools, and he had no predecessor to turn to for advice. Dr. H. J. Croot, who had been minister under the colonial government, was unlikely to be helpful as the conditions of work would be vastly different. He was grateful to the technical staff at the ministry who pulled together a few documents to guide his thinking. He quickly put together a team to draft the national health strategy for the newly independent Uganda.[7]

***

The days leading to 9 October, 1962, were memorable to Ugandans for many reasons. The excitement was palpable. It was akin to the expectation of the first serious downpour after a long dry spell, only more intense. All across the country, the independence storm broke forth with loud claps of thunder and lightning. While many rural Ugandans did not fully understand the significance of what was happening in faraway Kampala, with the lowering of the Union Jack and the triumphant ascension of the Ugandan flag, as bold and beautiful as the women that danced to the loud drumming throughout the night, those that had experienced the indignity and scorn of the colonial master up close knew freedom had come. Nowhere, perhaps, was the awareness of the difference between colonial master and servant sharper than within the medical fraternity.

***

Nkore worked as a senior clerk at the District Commissioner's office in Kabale. He had heard a lot about the independence plans. On the morning of 9 October 1962, just as he was preparing to leave the house, his pregnant wife quietly announced that the baby might be arriving the same day. "Really?" Nkore asked, not quite absorbing the full import of the information. The wife could tell that his mind was already out there in the Independence frenzy. Besides, what would he do to help even if he were home? Cane and hat in hand, Nkore was already half out of the door when he asked if she had alerted the midwife.

"Yes, she is aware."

"Good", and with that he was gone.

---

[7] New Vision. Lumu headed the best ever health system in Uganda. 17 April 2012

So, while the rest of the country was preoccupied with the Independence preparations and festivities, Mrs. Nkore's one thought was the imminent arrival of the baby. The friend and self-taught midwife that had helped her to deliver previous babies was on high alert, and had been for days. Both women knew it could not be too long now. By midmorning, however, all discomfort had subsided, and Mrs. Nkore thought she might have misread the signs. She went about her chores without any sign of labor. In the evening though, with hardly any warning, her waters broke. In a couple of hours she gave birth to a bouncing baby girl. Nkore returned long past midnight to find that the baby had arrived in his absence. "Of course the baby must be named 'Independence'," he exclaimed, as soon as he heard of the birth. Independence, or Kweetegyeka, in Rukiga. By the time the baby was a month old, nobody but the father used the whole name, considered too weighty for a tiny little baby. Everybody else called her Kweete.

On 16 October 1962, the New Mulago Hospital opened its doors amidst great pomp and fanfare. Queen Elizabeth's cousin, Her Royal Highness the Duchess of Kent, traveled to Uganda to officiate at the opening. Alderdice, a former Medical Superintendent of (the old) Mulago hospital, writing in the *Lancet* of August 1963, said this of the new hospital, "A 900-bed hospital has been constructed in Kampala, Uganda, of a standard that compares favorably with teaching hospitals of recent design elsewhere." With regard to the medical school, he was equally full of praise. "Throughout the course, standards obtaining in the best British medical schools apply. ... Library facilities for students and staff are of a very high standard. The Albert Cook library has the best collection in East Africa and very few journals to which a member of staff may wish to refer are not available."

***

> At Mulago the intention was to build a 750-bed general hospital (to which was later added a private wing of 130 beds). Once the figure of £2 million for the building, £220,000 for medical equipment, and £80,000 for an extension to the nurses' home was arrived at and voted by Parliament, the architect and the planning committee were determined to cut their cloth accordingly. Although experience elsewhere in Africa raised serious doubts about the adequacy of the money voted, the hospital was in fact completed and equipped virtually within this figure.
>
> Two factors helped to keep the costs within bounds. The first and more important was the speed with which the hospital was designed and building started: the whole project from the first sketch to completion took less than five years; and this gave less time for prices to rise. The second was the determination of the architect (who controlled expenditure and held the vote book) and the planning committee to keep within the figure set, even though this meant a good deal of give and take.
>
> A. A. Alderdice, M.B. Sydney, M.R.C.P. The New Mulago Hospital. *Lancet* August 3, 1963.

On 22 February 1966, Health minister Dr. Lumu had a premonition that the Cabinet meeting he was going to attend at State House would not end well. He nonetheless prepared a technical brief about the plans for the new regional hospitals in case he had to give an update. Political tensions had been rising, and allegiances had been shifting back and forth for months. Although the Uganda People's Congress had managed to build a clear majority in the legislative house, the party was deeply divided, and things were coming to a head. Minister of State Grace Ibingira had abandoned all subtlety as he sought to pull the rug from under Prime Minister Obote. Lumu had been in meetings with the Ibingira group, and they were beginning to feel confident of their advantage both in Parliament and in Cabinet. For his part, the Kabaka of Buganda and President of the republic, Sir Edward Mutesa, was considering pushing Obote out, and creating a new government. It would seem that he had gone so far as to seek the advice of Attorney General Godfrey Binaisa about the legal implications of removing Prime Minister Obote from office. Clearly, all of this plotting was not discrete enough, as Obote's checkmate move would soon reveal.

Driving through Entebbe town, Lumu noticed that there was unusually tight security. A bigger surprise awaited him at State House. He arrived to find that rather than the usual Cabinet meeting, there were only three other ministers waiting to meet the president: Mathias Ngobi, G.B.K Magezi, and Grace Ibingira. A fifth minister, Balaki Kirya, arrived shortly afterwards. Beyond the brief greetings, nobody spoke. Every man sat quietly with his own thoughts. Obote was seated in his usual spot. Sam Odaka, his personal assistant (aide-de-camp), was the only other person in the room. A soldier came into the room, and Obote asked the ministers to follow him. At the door they were met by soldiers who led them to a waiting van. Some seven hours later they were ushered into Patiko prison in Gulu, and later transferred to Kotido in Karamoja where they were imprisoned without trial. Seated in a remote prison in Karamoja, Dr. Lumu could not have felt more removed from his patients and students at Mulago. The purging of the Cabinet to remove the troublesome Ibingira and his group was not the end of the political headaches for Obote. It heralded more turbulence as Obote sought to consolidate his control and eliminate all possible threats to his presidency. On 30 April 1966 Obote announced a new Constitution which was passed without debate, and he was then promptly elected President under the new constitution.

President Milton Obote talking to Narendra Patel,
Speaker of the National Assembly. *DS Archives*

***

The operating rooms on the ground floor of Uganda's largest and most prestigious hospital were abuzz with activity. Thursday was the main theatre day for Red Firm, and Dr. Sebastian Kyalwazi, who had returned from Britain a year earlier, had a long list of patients lined up for surgery. It was said that he had been among the top students in the exams that saw him becoming a Member of the Royal College of Surgeons of Edinburgh. For many of the junior staff that was wonderful news, but it came with a fair amount of confusion. Was he now to be treated the way they treated Prof. Ian McAdam? Was he going to have special theatre gowns with his name on them? Up until that time only the white doctors had personalized gowns. The easy bit was his joining the white doctors in the surgeons' room, but these other privileges were still somewhat unclear. In that exclusive club Kyalwazi would soon be joined by another British trained Ugandan surgeon, Alexander Odonga.

In truth Kyalwazi and Odonga did not have to be as good as their British counterparts to attain membership to the Royal College of Surgeons. They had to be much better, in order to be considered as good. The door to the surgeons' room was very narrow indeed for the so-called natives, and the Ugandans that got in during those early days were resilient and especially brilliant. The struggle for equal professional recognition went as far back as the late 1930s, in fact for as long as the Africans had a role in 'modern' medical care other than that of being the patient.

Kyalwazi pushed through the main double-door entrance to the theatre and made an immediate left turn into the surgeons' changing room. Here the doctors would exchange their street clothes and clinical coats for special gowns, usually used only here. In a couple of minutes he had changed, and he exited the changing rooms directly into the main corridor within the theatre. There were six spacious operating rooms, each separated from the next by scrubbing bays, equipment storage, and trolley preparation space. Inside each theatre was a new operating table with special overhead lighting that incorporated a camera for televising operations. On one wall was a board on which the instrument nurse would record all the instruments on the trolley, and the number of mops and towels at the team's disposal. At the end of each procedure the nurse would do a loud count to be sure that no instruments or swabs were left in the wound. On the other wall was an X-ray viewer that allowed the surgical team to display any X-ray films that might be needed for the procedure. All theatres were fitted with piped oxygen and suction facilities.

Kyalwazi checked the board in the surgeon's room to confirm what theatre he had been assigned, and then made his way down to Theatre 2. The anesthetist was busy securing an intravenous line on the first patient. "*Maama, wasuze bulungi?*" he asked the patient. "How was your night?" He always made a point to talk to the patients before they were put to sleep.

***

> Karungi's earliest memory of Kweete was at a family gathering. It might have been a wedding or a funeral. They could not have been older than seven years. All the kids were running around, and Aunt

Adrine reminded them repeatedly that Kweete was not to run too fast or she would end up in the hospital. Kweete looked just fine to the other kids and so the warning fell on deaf ears. In a sea of children of all ages, three little girls were inseparable: Karungi, Biitu, and Kweete. Like Kweete, Biitu's full name was hardly remembered and rarely used. Few would have made the connection between it and the English royal name Beatrice. While Karungi and Kweete were first cousins, Biitu's family was from a different clan, although their homesteads were only a stone's throw apart. During the school holidays, Biitu would sometimes arrive at her friend's home early enough for breakfast, and she might not return to her own home until after supper. The parents had long stopped the threats and beatings that they had used to try to keep her away from Kweete and Karungi, who Biitu called Rungi. The parents should not have worried though. The only mischief the girls ever got into, if it was that, was to climb every fruit tree on the property. Otherwise, they usually spent the days playing hide and seek, '*kwepena*', marble games using riverbed stones, and hunting for guavas and other fruits. It was later, when the girls were nearly ten, that Kweete became critically ill, and had to spend nearly two months in hospital. The doctors determined that she had an infection involving the inner lining of her heart, on top of the asthma that had bothered her episodically since she was about four. Because she missed the most critical term of the school year, she had to redo the class, falling behind her peers by a whole year. For Karungi the following holiday was not much fun as Kweete could not climb trees, did not want to run around, and she absolutely could not play in the rain. These restrictions were to remain for the next several years. The following year Karungi's parents sent her off to boarding school, so her contact with her two soul mates was further curtailed.

With Rungi gone to boarding school and Kweete not well enough to join her in their usual escapades, Biitu now had no choice but to take on the chores and tasks that her mother insisted were essential for every girl's survival. She was taught how to peel *matoke* perfectly without looking, how to winnow and grind millet, and how to take care of little babies. Her mother told her this was the meaningful education, not the reading of books that had little to do with real life. Without Rungi and Kweete life was dull but not lacking in activity.

***

In the evening of 19 December 1969, Professor Ian McAdam, the Head of Department of Surgery, was just exiting the hospital when he heard on the car radio that President Obote had been shot at while leaving Lugogo sports stadium, where he had just closed the UPC annual delegates' convention. Usually by this time McAdam would already be at the club, but on Fridays he sometimes did an evening round to especially make sure the post-operative patients were comfortable, and to preempt calls late in the night. As he swung his car into Kira Road to head towards Mulago roundabout and on to the doctors' club, he saw a convoy speeding towards the hospital entrance from the opposite direction, sirens blaring. His sixth sense told him to turn around and head back into the hospital. By the time he made the full turn at the roundabout, the motorcade had disappeared into the hospital. He returned to the parking that he had just left on Level 3, and entered the hospital through the Casualty Department. The previously calm waiting area was busy. There were soldiers and police officers standing around, and although he had taken the precaution to put on his clinical coat, they would not let him take the lift. He walked straight through to the main staircase in the central block, and then ran up to the 6th floor, taking two steps at a time. As he came up to the landing he was met by the 6th floor Matron and two younger doctors.

"We have been trying to reach you", the Matron said, visibly relieved to see him.

"I heard the news on the radio. I was just leaving so I turned and came back."

"This way please. He is in Room 1." Room 1 on Ward 6B was the top VIP room. The entire floor had been cordoned off, and for the duration of the President's stay there were soldiers at the entrance, and the elevators were closely guarded.

Dr. Kyalwazi arrived shortly afterwards. The two surgeons reviewed the patient and ordered that he be taken to the theatre immediately. They then called Dr. Martin Aliker, the dental surgeon, to join them in theatre.

The stories from Lugogo were as varied and numerous as the people willing to tell them. Some said an assassin had taken a shot at the President as he emerged from the hall, but that the split second before he pulled the trigger, a super-alert Obote had spotted him and dived to the ground, which was how he survived. The bullets that followed, according this version of the story, were by his security as they both covered him and tried to take out the assassin. Others swore that Mr. President had really not survived a bullet, but had had a little too much to drink. They argued that any bullet that knocked out his teeth and injured his tongue would have ripped through his brain, or at the very least shattered the jaw. As it was, the news from the hospital was that the President was safe and stable. Obote himself insisted later that someone tried to kill him, and that he got broken teeth and a tear in the tongue from the gunshot. Over time the stories were laundered in bleach and dyed every color of the rainbow, so it was impossible to know what really happened. What was remarkable though, was that the head of state was rushed to Mulago, which at that time was synonymous with the highest level of medical care in the country, if not in the region. The time for presidents to move with their own emergency medical teams complete with an operating theatre on wheels, as was rumored to be the case with a later administration, and for evacuations to European capitals on the first sign of a medical ailment, was yet to come.

THE SCARY SEVENTIES

From East and West, From North and South
All voices singing, Arise Makerere
Rise up and rise, High up and high
All voices singing
Arise Makerere

Dr. Lumu's plan had stipulated that a 600-bed hospital would be constructed in each of the four regional headquarters: Mbale, Gulu, Fort Portal, and Masaka. Another 600-bed hospital was to be built in Kampala to relieve Mulago of congestion, and to allow the national referral hospital to serve its main functions of referral, teaching and research. The Amin presidency heralded uncertainty that escalated rapidly. In 1972, barely a year into the presidency, he expelled all the Asian doctors, creating a huge void in the capacity of the hospital and the medical school, literally overnight. A number of non-Asian senior doctors left shortly after, either in protest of the treatment meted out to their Asian colleagues, or for fear of the escalating violence. The heads of department of Surgery, Obstetrics and Gynecology, and Internal Medicine resigned and left in the same week. Amin's ministers of health, first Dr. Justin Gesa, and later Henry Kyemba, seemed to have been spinning around Amin's insanely unpredictable plans and demands that any serious intentions for the construction of the hospitals fell by the wayside. Despite the extreme violence that engulfed all professionals, Amin singled out the doctors and judges for unexpected favors. He gave senior consultants Mercedes Benzes, and other doctors got cars as well. As the self-declared economic war intensified and common commodities disappeared from the market, Amin created a special outlet for doctors in Industrial Area. From here, doctors would be allocated sugar, beer, salt, and rice at very low prices. Most doctors would turn around and sell the items to supplement their meagre incomes. Likewise, Amin had a fuel pump installed in Old Mulago close to the Polio Hostel for the exclusive use of doctors.

***

Military doctors everywhere enjoy respect from the men and women they serve, and in times of peace, recruits to such positions are attracted to the trappings of a military office without the risk of combat. Amin's army doctors would have been no different. They would have had many privileges that their civilian peers did not have – a furnished house, a car, a food allowance, and access to the army shop where they could buy commodities such as wine and whisky that were not readily available on the market. And for all that, the most they would have had to do was examine recruits, and treat minor ailments at the army clinic. For one such doctor (names withheld) life was not perfect, but he was not complaining. The military coup in January 1971 had not brought any change to his personal circumstances. Then things started to change. First, he was singled out during an officers' meeting as being the doctor. "Eh. *Daktari?*" the President had half asked, half stated, as though this was a curiosity. Then he started receiving calls to attend to patients whose injuries were clearly not accidental. Multiple fractures, black eyes, bruises all over the body, even burns. He saw most of these patients only once and never asked what happened to them after his one-off treatment sessions. He had to certify deaths whose causes were evidently unnatural. He was already sleeping poorly and having nightmares when the Commandant called him to his office and notified him that there were going to be executions, and that he would be required to certify that the men to be executed were in good health. Executions! His heart did a somersault and then started racing. He felt sick. He had not become a doctor to do this. Besides, if these men were going to be killed, what did it matter whether they had tuberculosis, gonorrhea, or were in perfect health? And once they were shot, why could the men assigned to do the deed not confirm for themselves that their mission had been accomplished? After all, Ugandans were being killed and buried every day without requiring that a doctor confirm their demise. But he had been in the army long enough to know that you did not question orders. He listened attentively, gave the required salute, and walked out of the Commandant's office with his stomach churning, and his tongue stuck to the roof of his dry mouth. A few years previously, an army officer that he knew well had been executed in Mbale. He had been tried by an army tribunal and found guilty of being a FRONASA[8] collaborator. Masaba had been a pleasant guy, and they had played darts together a few times. His execution had left the doctor quite depressed for some time.

***

Kweete was giddy with excitement at the prospect of traveling to Kampala. She had heard her father talk about the city, but she never imagined that she would one day see it with her own eyes. She and her brother Kwesiga, who everybody called Kwesi, often played games in which they were going to Kampala, and coming back with lots of goodies that they imagined were free for the taking once one got to the city. Kweete's cousin Karungi had been to Kampala. She traveled with her mother to her sister's wedding, at which she was a bridesmaid. When she returned, Kweete and Biitu were waiting to hear all about the city. They were disappointed. Karungi told them that they stayed in a place called Bukoto, and that her aunt's house was a flat. That was confusing – how was a house flat? Then the wedding happened at a big church, and the reception was at a big hotel near the church. Biitu wanted to know if she saw the President's house. She had not. Did she see the TV house? No. Did she see Lake Victoria? No. Biitu quickly concluded that Karungi's Kampala visit did not count. Now Kweete was about to go there, and she intended to make her visit count.

Kweete had been to Kisizi Hopsital for her routine review, and the *Mzungu* doctor who examined her talked to her father at length

---

[8] The Front for National Salvation (FRONASA) was a Ugandan rebel group formed by Yoweri Museveni in 1972. It was one of the 28 groups represented in a meeting in Moshi, Tanzania between 24 and 26 March 1979 in what would become known as the Moshi Conference. That meeting formed the Uganda National Liberation Front (UNLF) and its military wing the Uganda National Liberation Army (UNLA), to fight alongside Tanzanian forces against Idi Amin. UNLA and Tanzanian forces in the Uganda–Tanzania War led to the overthrow of Idi Amin›s regime.

afterwards. Kweete did not understand most of what was said as the white man's speech was hard to follow, but from what she could piece together, the doctors at Mulago Hospital in Kampala had come up with new ways of treating heart diseases such as she had. Kweete had waited for them to leave the hospital, but on the way home she could not contain her curiosity any longer.

"Father, what did the *Mzungu* say?"

"He thinks you are doing well. He has said that you should carry on with the medicines that you have been taking."

"Is that all?"

"He mentioned that there is a group of doctors in Mulago who are working very hard to find better ways of treating heart diseases. He thought it might be good idea for them to examine you as well."

"So are we going there?"

"Not right away. I need to discuss it with your mother, and to take leave from work to be able to take you. The doctor said it is not urgent, but if and when we do decide to go he will give us a letter to the doctors in Mulago."

Kweete had to be content with that, not knowing if they would ever go. That had been months ago. Then one night her father came home and announced that he and Kweete would be traveling to Kampala in the morning. He had the letter from the hospital, and as it happened, the hospital van was due to pick up supplies from Kampala, so they had offered to take them to Mulago on the same trip. Everything happened so fast. Kweete had no opportunity to tell her friends that she was going to Kampala. They would be so envious! Only Kwesi was there to wish he was going.

The Medical Outpatient Clinics at Mulago were located on the 4th floor of the hospital's front wing. There was a pharmacy at the entrance, and there were labs on site to do most of the basic tests needed by the doctors. Patients who did not need imaging could come in for care and leave without needing to get farther into the hospital. All the consultation rooms were designed with wide glass windows overlooking the car park, and the sun and fresh air made this a pleasant place to work, even considering that it was a hospital. Sr. Imelda Atim kept a very orderly clinic. Dr. Kibukamusoke liked to know as soon as he came in how many patients were booked, and if they had the latest lab results on file. He usually saw the new patients first, especially if they were referrals from upcountry. The child from Kabale was the first in line.

Eight o'clock came and went, as did 9 o'clock. This was unusual for Dr. Kibukamusoke to not be at the clinic on time, and more unusual still that he had not communicated about his absence. On the few occasions when he was unable to run the clinic, he let the staff know who would see his patients. At 9.30 am Atim called the doctor's office, and the telephone went unanswered. Atim walked to the Department of Medicine on the same floor and asked the Department secretary if she had seen Dr. Kibukamusoke. "No. I have not seen him this morning. You may want to check with Dr. D'Arbela in case he is teaching somewhere."

"He would have let us know. And I noticed his car is not at its usual spot. It seems like he has not come to the hospital at all. Could you please check if someone else has been assigned to see the patients? We have a full clinic."

It had been only three months since Kibukamusoke took over the headship of the department from Dr. Bill Parson who left in December 1972. By the following day, rumour had it that Dr. Kibukamusoke had left the country. Within a few weeks he was replaced by Dr. Paul D'Arbela, a physician with specialization in diseases of the heart, and one that had made major contributions to the training of specialist doctors at Makerere.

Kibukamusoke's departure was by no means unique. Some doctors walked off ward rounds to go to the bathroom, and did not return for decades, if ever. The less lucky were picked up by the State Research Bureau agents, never to be seen again. Dr. D'Arbela's succeeding Kibukamusoke as department head was the easy part. The more difficult assignment proved to be that of personal physician to the Head of State, Field Marshal Idi Amin Dada. Very early on in that role, D'Arbela found out that his predecessor's woes had stemmed from his attempt to monitor and treat the President's gout problems. The repeated requests for urine samples worried Amin. He feared that he was being poisoned through the urine. Too paranoid to place his health in the hands of one doctor, Amin had secured the services of an Egyptian doctor on the side. With this knowledge, D'Arbela played it very safe. He made all his prescriptions sound like mere suggestions, knowing that Amin would discuss them with the Egyptian physician, who would very likely issue the same instructions D'Arbela would have given. With this delicate triangular relationship between suspicious patient, cautious doctor, and trusted expatriate back-up, D'Arbela was able to survive Amin's presidency. His unceremonious exit would come later through a different avenue. For the moment, his biggest preoccupation, and that of his senior colleagues, was how to maintain and even expand the teaching and medical services despite the continuing exodus of highly trained staff.

"Kibukamusoke had taken over as acting Department Head from Bill Parson who left in the first wave of departures after Amin expelled the Asians," D'Arbela recalled. "When Kibukamusoke left, I was asked to head the department. The Master of Medicine program had been started in 1968 under Parson, and we had to sustain it. Olweny and Kiire were among the first batch from that program. I quickly assigned the promising young doctors to various specialties – Otim to endocrinology, Batambuze to cardiology, there was Mugerwa, Kiwanuka … We ensured that there was succession and continuity of the programs. It was the Masters of Medicine programs that saved the medical school from collapse."

Drs. Krishna Somers and Paul D'Arbela conducted most of the original research on endomyocardial fibrosis, a disease of obscure cause, which leads to heart failure in the extreme. When the New Mulago opened in 1962, the medical school received a £10,000 grant (equivalent to £160,000 [UGX881 million] in September 2019) from the National and

Grindlays Bank in Kampala. With this, they bought equipment for the heart laboratory.[9]

***

If the hospital suffered a shortage of doctors, the Medical School was probably even more acutely affected. The biomedical sciences of anatomy, physiology and biochemistry were practically depleted of senior staff. Lab technicians were in some instances taking on the roles of the teaching staff. Anthony Gakwaya, an undergraduate in the early seventies, recalled that the class spent almost a year in the biochemistry class discussing the DNA structure which had been discovered by James Watson and Francis Crick some twenty years earlier. Gene sequencing was still very topical, and Frederick Sanger and others were still racing to see who would be the first to discover a method of rapidly ordering – sequencing – the building blocks of proteins. Ugandan medical students were facing an uncertain future with few teachers and hardly any lab reagents, but they were doing what they could to stay in the mainstream of knowledge. The Albert Cook Library that had enjoyed great prestige, and that had subscriptions to a wide variety of scientific journals, could no longer keep up. First there was a slowing down, then the deliveries stopped altogether.

In a span of a few years, student life at Makerere changed from one of relative luxury to one of great hardship. Where the halls of residence had been the envy of even the working class around Kampala, now they were often plunged in darkness from frequent power outages, and water was erratic. Food quality suffered, and was the cause of a few strikes in the early Amin years, before it became evident that the problems facing the nation were far graver than poorly cooked meals. Military presence on Makerere campus became commonplace, and the insecurity that had engulfed the rest of the city now extended to the hill that prided itself in being the seat of independent thinking and academia. The stage was set for a violent confrontation.

---

[9] Heart catheterization was being done in Mulago, and nowhere else in East and Central Africa. Somers and D'Arbela taught cardiology to a pioneer class of 12 students, including Drs. Charles Olweny, Peter Lobo, John Babigumira, Ashvin Patel, Justine Lwanga, and Lamech Mwanje. Others would later follow, including Ephraim Batambuze, Marcel Otim, and Thomas Ogada.

Olive Kobusingye

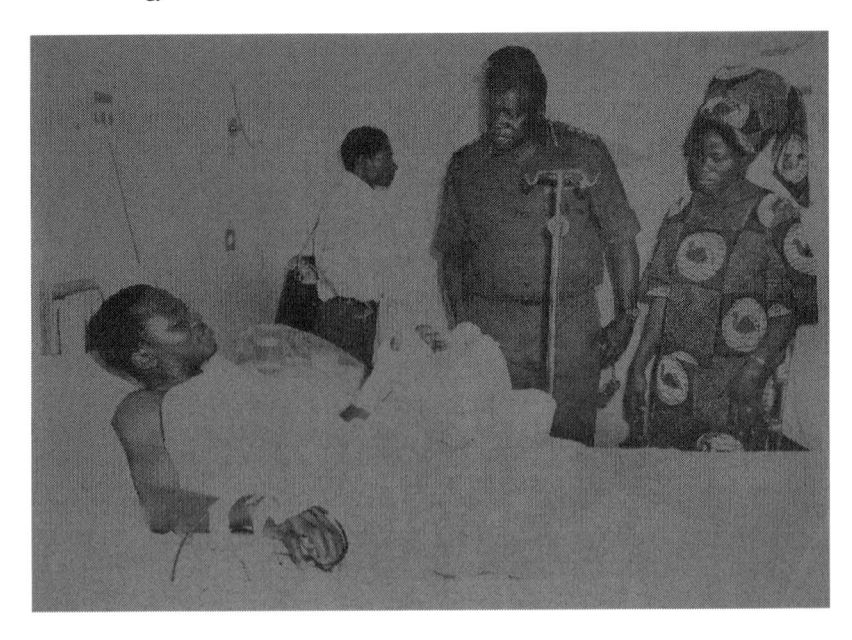

President Idi Amin Dada visits Mulago Hospital at its
10th Anniversary, 16 October 1972. *DS Archives*

***

On the night of 27 June 1976, Dr. Adam Kimala, Provincial Medical Officer for North Buganda Province, was driving from Mityana to Lugazi when he ran into a big military convoy at Kibuye. He gave the convoy a wide berth and continued his journey undisturbed. The following day he learnt that an Air France plane had been hijacked and landed at Entebbe, and he thought that might explain the military presence on Entebbe road. As the situation evolved, most of the hostages were released, except for some 106 passengers who were either Israelis, or non-Israeli Jews. The hijackers were trading their lives for the release of terrorists held in prisons mostly in Israel, but also in some European countries. All this remained remote to Kimala, whose responsibilities as both the provincial head of the medical services and the Medical Superintendent of Kawolo Hospital kept him busy enough. But fate was about to hand Kimala a strange assignment.

As he recounted, "One morning that week, a Police detective from Lugazi called me to say that they had found a dead body, and I was required to go and do a postmortem. The body was in a sugar plantation in Namawojjolo along Jinja Road. When we got to the body, I examined it, and noted that it was burnt. There was a burn in some sort of straight line from the head to the legs, a pattern unlikely in a live person who would be struggling, suggesting that the burn was inflicted after death. I could see that it was a short white female, probably in her sixties or seventies. I quickly came to the conclusion that this was not a simple murder, and that someone had killed the woman and wanted to hide her identity, or the mode of her death, probably both. Given the circumstances, I thought it best to not make a detailed report. Something told me this body was going to cause us problems. It was dangerous. I wrote a very short report, and said the body was burnt beyond recognition. We sent for prisoners from Lugazi prison and they buried the body right there in the plantation. I gave the Police officer the short report, and went back to the hospital, hoping that was the end of the matter."

It was not. In a day or so, news broke that one of the hostages, Dora Bloch, had been killed, and that her body had been dumped in Namanve. Kimala began to worry in earnest. He consoled himself that he had not been near Namanve. He prayed that the Police detective and the prisoners would keep their mouths shut. He did not have to wait for long to discover that people could not keep secrets. A few mornings after the postmortem, Kimala was walking to one of the wards when security officers came into the hospital. They asked him for the Medical Superintendent's office. "I pointed them to my office. As they headed there, I got into the car, and drove to Bugerere. I told my staff that I had to supervise work in the Province - Kyaggwe, Bulemeezi, and Mubende. Three times, the security officers came to my office and did not find me. They searched my office. They went to my home and asked my wife if she knew of my whereabouts. They wanted to know if I had brought any reports home recently. She knew what they were after. She told them that she had heard me talking of a report that I had deposited at the Police. They went straight there and they were given the report. One of them returned and told my wife to let me know that everything was okay, that I had given a good report. After that they never came back."

***

The date for the execution was set as 9 September 1977. The men to be executed had been tried by an army tribunal and found guilty of various crimes, including plotting to overthrow the government of President Idi Amin, being economic saboteurs, and spying. The program was quite elaborate. The government radio station had aired announcements of the planned executions, and the public was invited to come and witness how enemies of the state were punished. On D-day the prisoners were brought to the Kampala Clock Tower grounds in the Prisons Department vans. They were blindfolded and frog-marched, each to a metallic pole set up for the purpose, where they were tied. An army officer moved from pole to pole ascertaining that they were all properly secured. The soldiers to execute the prisoners lined up with their guns at the ready. The army chaplain was then invited to come and give the men their final benediction, or whatever spiritual comfort he could impart in the grim circumstances. At exactly 4 o'clock the officer in charge of the execution gave the single command to fire, and the shots were discharged, each prisoner stopping three shots directed to the head. After that the doctor, who had been in attendance from the beginning, came forward to confirm that the men were indeed dead. He had been so anguished by having to participate in the executions that he did not think through exactly how he was going to confirm the deaths of the men, shot at close range only moments before. As he approached the poles he suddenly realized he had no tools, and in the same moment realized the absurdity of the very thought of tools. One of the bodies was all but decapitated. He moved along the line barely touching the bodies, although it occurred to him that he could perhaps try to feel for their carotid pulses. He was relieved that the men assigned to remove the bodies were following quickly in his wake, cutting the lifeless bodies off the poles, and placing them in coffins. He did not recall how he left the Clock Tower grounds. He did not recall who he talked to, if anyone. He somehow managed to make it back to his house in Makindye where he downed one *Uganda waragi* glass after another until he passed out on his living room floor.

***

In 1979 when Amin's government fell, Kimala was back in Mulago training to be a surgeon. The Israeli government requested Uganda to help locate Dora Bloch's remains. Kimala led the team that located and exhumed the body. "I could remember where the body was buried. We dug up the bones. Benjamin Bloch, Dora's son, had brought with him her medical records to help with the identification. Based on some documented dental work, and an implant in her vertebra, we were able to make a positive identification. It was a somber moment, but the son appreciated that we were able to find his mother's remains. He took them and she was given a proper burial back home in Israel."

THE ENIGMATIC EIGHTIES

Do not forget, through all the years
Those who have gone through the gates of Makerere
Give them the pride, Give them the joy
Oh! To remember, the gates of Makerere

The first weeks of medical school went by in a flash. Everything was new. While the students in other faculties carried on partying as was the custom at the beginning of every academic year, the medical students plunged into serious study. Every morning the medics walked from Makerere main campus across the valley to Mulago, mostly through Katanga valley. The cadaver room was the center of the new class. Small groups of five or six students were each assigned a cadaver. The introductory lecture in Anatomy was on the breast, but nobody called it that. Here in Anatomy it was the mammary gland. The arm, also called the upper limb, was more appropriately called the brachium. It was here that the seeds of complete language alteration were sowed, so that in future the doctors would think that *pedal edema* communicated better than swelling of the feet, and that *epistaxis* was clearer than nasal bleeding. It was here in the cadaver room that fears were overcome, and that lifelong relationships developed. There was something comforting about discovering that the smartest sounding guys did not necessarily have the steadiest hands at dissection, and that some unassuming students with thick rural accents had incredible capacity to memorize endless random facts about the human body. In a few weeks, everyone was comfortable in the company of the cadavers, which were slowly but surely being taken apart layer by chloroform infused layer. Prof.

Sebuwufu said these were the students' first patients, and they were to take good care of them. Dr. A. Galloway, the first head of the Department of Anatomy, would have been impressed.

Some organs were described as being pear or almond shaped although there was not one pear tree in all of Uganda, and God help the student who dared to liken them to an avocado, a fruit the students and their teachers saw and ate on a regular basis. The normal ovary was said to be almond shaped. The students had never seen an almond, and the ovaries in the cadavers were anything but normal, so their imagination of what an almond looked like would have to do. In the clinical years there would be other curiosities, such as the cobblestone appearance of a trachoma eye membrane. No student had seen real life cobblestones, and perhaps neither had some of their teachers, but cobblestone it would be. Then there was the classic anchovy sauce appearance of an amoebic liver abscess. For goodness' sake, what was an anchovy? The descriptions tended to obscure rather than illuminate. The height of obscurity was perhaps the '*café au lait*' spots, which would have been familiar had someone told the students that the exotic sounding phrase was French for milky coffee. Students that had not been within thousands of miles of any snow were taught how to recognize a diseased lung by a 'snow storm' appearance on the radiograph. The endless hours in the cadaver room, the physiology lab, and the wards that the students would graduate to after two years of basic sciences, ensured that their new language took firm root. Karungi, by nature generously endowed with a curiosity for words and languages, soaked up – or rather, imbibed – this new language like a sponge.

'Science should speak the language of the common people' Rudolf Karl Ludwig Virchow, nineteenth-century German physician (1821-1902).

***

The post-mortem room – PM room – was cooler than the rest of the hospital, being adjacent to the refrigerators that contained what the

Pathology professor called the teachers. "The dead teach us many things. They make us wise if we take the time to study them. They come here carrying many secrets. Every dead body is a wealth of wisdom. So – open them up with respect. Look. Feel. Here in this room the dead speak. This is the House of Wisdom." More often than not Prof. Wamukota said this while shaking the ash off the end of a cigarette. He probably used one matchstick a day, because he always lit the next cigarette off the butt of the one he was snuffing out. It did not matter that he saw many deaths from tobacco related diseases. He always said it was a pity for one to die with clean lungs. "Look! Clean as can be. This girl never smoked a cigarette, and very likely never cooked on a charcoal stove either. No trace of smoke. But what use are her lungs now?" Prof. Wamukota called every female a girl, no matter how old they were. "This girl of seventy five years came to the hospital with a cough, night fevers, and weight loss…" It always drew chuckles, but one had to be careful to not be seen laughing, because then one became the target for his caustic humor and ridicule. "Yes, you Nsereko. Come and tell us what you see here. Is that a normal liver?" A bony black forefinger tapped ash off the end of the almost finished cigarette, and brought it back to equally black lips, eyes barely open through the cloud of smoke, but clearly seeing enough to decipher the secrets hidden away in the dead woman's liver. The PM sessions were optional, and they took place during lunch hour, but one missed them at one's peril. They were introduced in the late 1940s by the first head of Pathology, Prof. Jack Davies, and had survived the many changes in location and management over the decades. The cold grey concrete slabs on which the bodies lay, the strong formaldehyde smell, the solid swing doors that separated this area from the rest of the hospital – this was probably the way things were when the mortuary was moved here in 1962.

Most of Prof. Wamukota's exam questions came from his lunchtime sessions, so they were well attended. From here it was rumored that he would make his way to Katanga, an infamous slum sprawled between Makerere and Mulago hills where cheap alcohol and even cheaper women waited for university students and professors alike. There was a running joke that a student who frequented Katanga walked into an oral exam, and the professor looked him up and down before asking, "So – apart from the bar, have we ever met anywhere?" Needless to say, the student failed the exam. The vivas, or oral exams, were by far the most dreaded form of assessment. The student was supposed to be rattled, baited with ambiguous questions, and humiliated for being ignorant. The questions were sometimes about obscure conditions to elicit even more obscure answers. It was not uncommon for a student to be asked about a disease condition that they had never come across in their three years of diligent clinical rotations, and to emerge from the viva in tears. Even in this, the students kept their humor. The more vicious and mean examiners were said to be malignant. The more reasonable, and those that asked about conditions that the student was most likely to encounter in the treatment of everyday patients, were said to be benign. Malignant or benign though, those senior doctors were wholly committed to turning their students into doctors that they could be proud of, and they spared no effort in doing that.

***

Having left Makerere medical school for Rubaga Hospital, D'Arbela had a comfortable routine that rotated between time spent at Rubaga, and an upscale private clinic on Clement Hill Road in Nakasero. One afternoon he was in his office at the clinic when his head nurse burst in and told him to get out. "Leave now. They are looking for you." D'Arbela had had the sense that he was under surveillance. It was rumored that he was supplying the NRA rebels with medicines using the cover of his clinic. He knew that many people did not get a second warning. He slipped out through the back while the security officers were at the reception asking about him. He had left his car in front of the clinic though, so he had to make the split second decision to either make a dash for it, or abandon it and find some other way to leave the area. He decided to get to his car.

D'Arbela was just pulling out when the soldiers came out the clinic. He hit the accelerator and sped away, but he knew the clock was now ticking for him. He was due for sabbatical at the Medical School, so kept his head low for a couple of days, bought a ticket, and left the country without ceremony. His first stop was London where he was no stranger, having trained at Hammersmith Hospital. He would later move to Saudi Arabia and make that his home for the next several years. Back home the exodus of health workers continued, each with their own unique story. It would be several years before he returned.

***

Dr. Bwogi Kanyerezi was head of the Department of Medicine when Dr. Obache, one of his colleagues, came to see him with a worrying story. Obache said he had been told by a close relative that some soldiers were planning to harm him. The relative was married to someone who worked as a secretary at the Army headquarters, and she had overheard some conversations. He had laughed it off the first time he heard about the threat, but the night before he had come home to find a strange car parked close to his gate. In the morning, he had noticed the same car at the end of the street as he drove out, and it had followed him to the hospital entrance. Although the car had civilian number plates he thought he saw some people in military uniform in his rear view mirror.

"Obache, if you feel threatened, get out. Do not wait. We can give you a leave of absence until things get better," Kanyerezi urged.

The following day Obache returned with an update. "I have been offered military protection. I now have a tent full of soldiers in my compound. They are going to protect me."

"You trust these people?" Kanyerezi was incredulous. "What are you doing here? How can you trust soldiers to protect you? You are not a soldier. Obache, just get away."

"I think I am now okay. I have been assured that I will be safe." Obache looked more relaxed than the day before, and the two doctors parted and went about their day's business.

Three days later Obache was killed in his house in Kololo. The soldiers that were supposed to ensure his personal safety were nowhere in sight when the killers came. From what his colleagues and relatives could piece together, Obache was considered a traitor by his Langi kinsmen. He had stayed in the country and thrived during Amin's time when all the Langi, particularly the elite, were being hunted down. His wife had worked as a secretary to the Minister of Finance under Amin.

Kanyerezi's turn to flee came through bizarre circumstances only a few weeks later. The end of term exams in the Department of Medicine had concluded without incident. Results were displayed in the usual manner, and the students who had not passed were required to repeat the rotation. Four months later, someone reported that the Department of Medicine had "failed UPC students." There was no way the lecturers could have arranged this even if they had wanted to, because they did not know which students had what political leanings. The accusation was initially dismissed, but an insider revived it and escalated it directly to Vice President Paulo Muwanga.

"Who is this Kanyerezi, to think he can just fail UPC students? We shall teach him a lesson," Muwanga said. One of the people present when Muwanga was told about the UPC students' examination results sought to alert Kanyerezi that he was now a marked man. The information eventually got to him the following day. He did not need much persuasion, remembering the fate of his colleague Obache. He drove home, prepared his family as best he could for such an abrupt departure, and around 7pm he drove out of his gate despite the nighttime curfew that was in effect. Because he did not have a better plan yet, he drove from his home in Rubaga to neighboring Lungujja and the whole family spent the night with friends. "A couple of hours after we left the house, a military truck full of soldiers drove up to the gate. Finding that there was nobody at home, they shot several rounds of ammunition in the air and left."

Over the next three weeks, Kanyerezi either lay low or moved with great stealth. A friend took him to see a sympathetic Member of Parliament who was also a Major in the army, to find out just how grave the situation was. Major Angwa offered to get him military protection. "No thank you! I will take my chances without their help." He reached out to the university Vice Chancellor, Prof. Asavia Wandira, explained his predicament, and let him know that the department was going to need a new head. He moved the family to a different location every few days to avoid being tracked down by the security agents. Through a network of friends, he secured help with escape plans. In the end, he left the country in a UNICEF vehicle that was destined for Kenya to pick up supplies. His wife followed soon after in the same manner.

Dr. Charles Olweny was already heading the Uganda Cancer Institute, now he took over as Head of Department of Medicine as well. Four and a half decades later, Olweny could still vividly remember how he became head of the Cancer Institute.

"In 1972 I was at the National Cancer Institute in the USA doing a Fellowship in Oncology. Six months to the end of the Fellowship a message came from Uganda. 'You should return to Uganda immediately. If you delay your return there will be nothing to return to.' Back home, Amin had expelled Asians, and many other expatriates had started to leave. All eight expatriate staff at the Uganda Cancer Institute were leaving. I wound up my stay prematurely and headed home. On arrival I reported to Kibukamusoke, who was Head of Medicine. He told me to go and talk to Prof. Kyalwazi. Kyalwazi was in Surgery, but had closer dealings with the Cancer Institute because of his research in liver cancer and Kaposi sarcoma. I went to see Kyalwazi, and told him that I could not head the Cancer Institute. 'The Institute has just lost all its senior staff. I don't think I can manage,' I told him. Kyalwazi held my hand. 'Son,' he said, 'you can do it. I will support you.' Two expatriate colleagues were waiting to hand over the Institute. As soon as I showed up they effected the hand-over, wished me well, and left. To his word, every Wednesday without fail, Kyalwazi came to the Institute to do rounds with me, and to help me think through any issues I needed help with."

Olweny lasted much longer than his predecessors in Medicine, but by 1983 when he left under the guise of a sabbatical, he was living like a fugitive, often having to spend nights in different locations to avoid 'disappearing' under the cover of darkness. These men were among the forerunners of the generation of Ugandan doctors that would go ahead to have illustrious medical careers while scattered in the diaspora. Despite the great odds, the Cancer Institute gave the world the first evidence that lymphomas (cancers of the lymphatic system) in all ages could be treated successfully with chemotherapy. Amidst scarcity, Olweny pioneered the concept of an essential drugs list, which concept was adopted by the World Health Organisation for use globally.

***

David Kisumba was the first Ugandan professor of orthopedics, attaining this status at a relatively young age. The reason few people know of him is that he died a truly untimely and premature death in a road traffic crash in Kololo, then a posh quiet neighborhood north of Kampala central business district. Nevertheless, he left an impression on his young nephew Mutyaba, who determined that he would be an orthopedic surgeon as well. The aspiration would have died the death of many such youthful dreams had his ambition not met with providence in the names of Professor Rodney Belcher, an American Navy flight surgeon who fell in love with Uganda. Belcher was no stranger to East Africa. He had started in Dar es Salaam as professor of surgery in the 1970s. In 1983, he came to Makerere as a Fulbright lecturer, but the country was in the throes of a full scale civil war, and he was forced to relocate to Nairobi. He was so committed to working in Uganda though, that as soon as the war ended in 1986 he started planning his return. Return he did, to a badly run down Mulago Hospital, where there were no orthopedic services to speak about, and where all surgical services were a major struggle.

Belcher realized that the care of the diseases of the bones and joints was always going to lag behind unless a department was created, where specialists could be trained. He was going to begin from the ground up. Mutyaba, who already had his general surgical training under his belt, was his first student. They needed a ward, an operating room, consulting rooms, classrooms ... they needed a lot of infrastructure that did not exist in post-war Mulago in 1988. What did exist though, that came to their aid, was a dilapidated bungalow in Old Mulago that housed patients with disabilities, mainly from polio. Having identified the house as a potential base, Belcher had to find the money. For this he turned to his old friends from his Airforce days. One of them was now a Senator, and Belcher thought he might find a way to get his dream department funded. He went back home, asked around, and then decided that Mutyaba would be helpful in telling their story. Before long Mutyaba was on the plane to the US to work with Belcher on a proposal that would hopefully get funded through his Senate connections. Their hard work paid off. A War Victims Fund had just been established, and the Belcher-Mutyaba proposal talked of helping to treat the huge backlog of both veterans and civilians that had been injured during the five-year civil war in Uganda. With time, the money came, and the Department of Orthopedics was born.

***

Kweete had been on the antenatal ward for a week already. She had been admitted for observation, and to ensure that she would get specialist attention when she went into labour. So far, her pregnancy had not worsened her heart condition as had been feared. She did not know what to expect, this being her first pregnancy.

By 1986 Flavia Katende had been a tutor and midwife in Mulago for more than a decade. In that time, she had taught several generations of nurses and medical students to deliver babies safely. Yet every year there was some additional form of improvisation. She remembered that during her own training it would have been unacceptable for there to be only one health worker at a delivery. The doctor or midwife usually had a receiving nurse, so that once the baby was out, the receiving nurse took care of the baby while the midwife ensured that the placenta, or afterbirth, was delivered safely. They gave the mother *ergometrine* injection to reduce the bleeding, and gently rubbed the abdomen to encourage the uterus to contract, further reducing the bleeding from the placenta bed. The midwife or attending doctor did not leave the mother's side until the bleeding had stopped, and the mother was clean and comfortable. Katende was aware that on some nights only one midwife was on duty in the maternity unit, assisted by inexperienced student nurses that were still terrified of the thought of cutting through skin and flesh. Delivery sets, the collection of instruments and supplies that one had to have in order to perform a safe delivery, had dwindled to a pair of rewashed gloves, old needle forceps, a blunt reusable needle, and loose cotton swabs. She had finally stopped giving her teaching on how to prepare for a normal delivery, because she could not bring herself to go through what were clearly fictitious lists. Students would never have seen the entire set anyway.

The evening of 25 January 1986 the maternity unit was unusually quiet. Lately the insecurity around Mulago had reached such levels that patients who did not come in before dark could not come in until the following morning. For some that would be too late. Katende would have gone home already but she was concerned about the teenager on the corner bed who was unlikely to have a normal delivery. She was the textbook high risk *prime gravida*, or first time pregnant: short frame, narrow pelvis, and baby's head high above the pelvis despite the increasing contractions. Katende usually told young doctors to be aware of this 'failure to progress' in labor, and to plan intervention sooner rather than later, as a normal delivery was unlikely and unsafe. The doctors always took the decisions, but the more experienced midwives could tell which patients were not going to make it on their own. Katende knew the teenager was headed for a C-section, but there was no anesthetist in the theatre. There were no doctors either.

***

The war had been advancing from Luweero towards Kampala for a long time, and in many people's minds this was how things were always going to be, but the last one month had been different. It was becoming clear that the guerrillas – '*abayeekera*' – were going to enter the city, and that the government forces were not able to stop them. The day before the gunfire had been so close that the midwives joked that they did not need to deliver the babies – they were popping out at the sound of the shootings. But today was strangely quiet. The Senior House Officer and the interns should have been here. If they were not in the hospital by now, they were not coming. What was she to do with the young mother? Then there was the patient with heart disease as well. These two were going to need doctors.

***

Kweete went into labour in the night. The labour progressed without incident and at dawn she gave birth to a baby boy, assisted by two student midwives. Shortly after birth the baby started turning blue, a sign that he was not getting enough oxygen into his blood. The nurses took the baby to the nursery where newborn babies received more intensive care. A few hours later the tragic news came – despite the doctors' best efforts, the baby had died. The doctors said there were serious defects in his heart and major blood vessels which were incompatible with life. Kweete was plunged into the depths of grief. She declined to have a post mortem done, and chose to bury her baby 'without him being turned into a specimen'. As the country started to cautiously celebrate the victory of the NRA and the end of the bush war, Kweete mourned the death of the baby that had barely lived.

***

Professor Francis Omaswa was coming back to Mulago after a hiatus of more than 10 years. For three years, he had headed the Cardiothoracic Department at Kenyatta Hospital in Nairobi. He had just spent five years at Ngora Hospital in eastern Uganda, and he could hardly wait to get back into heart surgery at a big hospital. But Mulago had scars and wounds from years of abuse and neglect, and he was about to find out the hard way that fixing a hospital could be harder than fixing hearts. It felt great walking along familiar corridors, running specialist clinics, and deciding what patients to schedule for surgery. His first heart operation was a straight forward one, the surgery went well, and the patient was taken to the Intensive Care Unit on 3D as planned. At the end of the day, Omaswa went by to see how he was doing, and was pleased to find him stable. The hospital was quickly emptying out, and the evening shift was giving way to the night staff. The big hospital routines were all very familiar.

The following morning Omaswa went to the ICU to check on the patient before heading to the ward for a teaching round. An unpleasant surprise awaited him. His stable patient of the previous evening had passed away in the night. The night team was gone, and there were scanty notes to explain how a patient that had done well at table and for the following several hours suddenly made a turn for the worst. That was not a good start, but Omaswa was not so easily discouraged. A week later he had another patient scheduled, and it was another fairly routine heart procedure. This time he gave more elaborate instructions, and went over them with the nurses in ICU to be sure that nothing would be missed. Before he left the hospital in the evening he want by the ICU, and was happy with the patient's condition. He lived just above Galloway House within Mulago, and he told the nurses to call him if there were any serious concerns. Decades later, Omaswa still recalled how things evolved.

"I was relieved that there were no calls in the night, as that meant that the patient had had a comfortable night. In the morning, I walked to 3D ICU to see the patient. As soon as I walked into the ward, I sensed that there was a problem. The procedure room was open and I could see there was a body behind a screen. As I turned to head towards the room where I had left the patient, the matron came out of the office. She did not waste any time. 'Professor, I am sorry but your patient died.' I stood still and felt a tightening in my chest. 'How? When?' I asked the questions, but somehow did not hear the answers. I knew it had to be the nursing care. There was nothing worrisome or highly complex about the procedures, I had done these same operations countless times before, and never had deaths. I turned and walked out of ICU without looking at the file. I walked down to the second floor, out into the parking, and I got into the car. A plan was quickly forming in my head, and the painful lumps in my chest and throat were not shifting. I knew I had to find a solution. A short while later I drove out of Mulago and headed straight to Nsambya Hospital. I walked into Dr. Duggan's office and told her secretary that I had to talk to her, and that it was urgent. I got straight to the point. 'I am looking for a hospital where to do heart surgery. I would do a weekly list.' She must have heard the pain in my voice. Or maybe there were tears in my eyes. She was quiet for a while, then she simply said yes. I thanked her, and said I would be back to work out the details.

From Nsambya I drove to Nakasero, to Dr. Ruhakana Rugunda's office. He was Minister of Health at the time. I still had the sense of urgency, and I told him I needed premises for a unit where we could treat patients with heart problems. I had walked around Mulago looking for space before, but that day I had an urgency like fire under my feet. I had to find a way to treat patients safely. That second death had rattled me pretty badly. I was angry and depressed all at once. Rugunda listened to me, and asked if I had suggestions. 'Yes. There are some old buildings in Old Mulago that accommodated internally displaced people from Luwero during the war. I think those people have left.' He said we could have the buildings. I walked out of there elated. In one morning I had a theatre in Nsambya where I could start work right away, and a couple of houses where I could set up a heart unit as a more permanent solution. The question was now how to find the money to get the unit together."

Rotarian Robert Ssebunya had been in exile in Nairobi, and he had seen the work of the Kenya Heart Foundation. On returning home after the 1986 change in government, he set about creating the Uganda Heart Foundation fashioned after the Kenyan one. Omaswa had been a natural ally, and the two had had several meetings with a few other people to give direction to the Foundation. It was to this group that Omaswa now turned to find the resources to give life to his dream. Some wealthy Asian patients made contributions, but the grant that really set them firmly on their way was US$350,000 from Rotary International. They renovated the dilapidated buildings and turned them into wards, built and equipped the operating theatre, bought a top-of-the-range Echocardiogram, and recruited staff. The Uganda Heart Institute was born. The rest was paperwork.[10]

---

[10] In 1988, four entities (Mulago Hospital, Ministry of Health, Makerere University and Uganda Heart Foundation) met at Mulago Hospital, and formally resolved to establish the Uganda Heart Institute. Cardiac services resumed on 4 April 1996 with the implantation of an External Pacemaker. In 2001 the Uganda Heart Institute was legally established as a company limited by guarantee to enable it to solicit for funds and manage its resources independent of Mulago. On 27 December 2007, open heart surgery resumed at Mulago. It had been forty years since the last such procedure was done here.

Prof. Paul D'Arbela, first Ugandan cardiologist.
Monitor Publications Limited.

Prof. Josephine Namboze (first Ugandan female medical graduate 1959). Makerere University School of Public Health 2019.

Olive Kobusingye

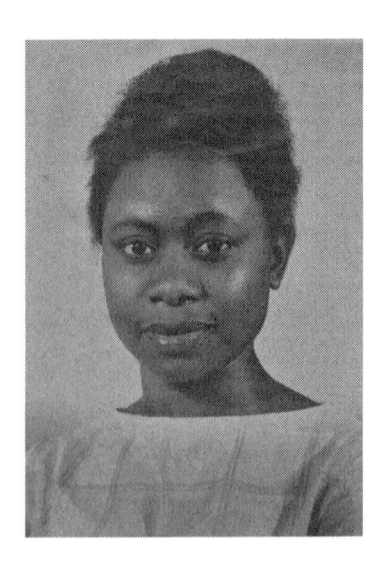

Dr. Rosemary Bagenda (second Ugandan female medical graduate 1965) *DS Archives*

Prof. Charles Olweny, first Ugandan Head of Uganda Cancer Institute. *Prof. Olweny*

***

The Patient

Prof. Richard Bwogi Kanyerezi. *Monitor Publications Limited.*

Prof. Sebastian Kyalwazi, first Ugandan surgeon.

Prof. Ian McAdam. *Albert Cook Library, College of Health Sciences, Makerere University*

On 20 December 1988, President Museveni visited Mulago Hospital. The staff of the hospital gathered in Davies Lecture Theatre to listen to him. The President was dapper in a stylish suit and tie and, if a little cocky in his speech, had an infectious optimism about him. This was the boardroom president; the bush guerrilla fighter was gone. He captivated the nurses and doctors with his plans, which reflected a passion for the rapid development of the country, after decades of mismanagement and neglect.

"We must have this capacity," he said. "Capacity to build houses, roads, stores, dams … railways. I am building a railway construction unit. I am using the Kasese line as an opportunity to build a railway construction unit. We must build the railway ourselves." Every eye was on the President's face, hanging onto his every word. "You know when we [National Resistance Army] came, we found that they [Obote's government] had a plan to get USD200 million to lay the rails. I asked them what exactly the money was

The Patient

for. I said, 'Two hundred million dollars is a lot of money. Tell me - exactly what are you going to do with this money? To lay iron bars from here to Kasese on a firm base?'" Museveni laughed. The audience chuckled in agreement. "If the British could build a railway from Mombasa to here in 1900, why is it so difficult for us now? So I said, no, let us look at the figures. And you know what? Most of that money was not going into the rails. It was going into building toilets, houses … I said, no! This must stop!"

The medics were impressed with a president that interrogated the figures. They could well imagine how he was going to move from the railway to the waste and neglect in the health system. Many of them were already imagining better equipped operating rooms. A revamped intensive care unit. A stable electricity supply. Better salaries. Stephen Kijjambu, a young surgeon who had already seen his fair share of dysfunction and scarcity, was filled with optimism. Museveni's talk was music to his ears. If the British were able to build Mulago from nothing in the late 1950s, he thought, how could the renovation and equipping of the hospital be so difficult now? The senior doctors who had held up the services against great odds were relieved. Although the new leaders were in military uniform, they understood and were committed to development. Some of the new leaders in uniform were doctors – notably, Dr. Ronald Bata and Dr. Kizza Besigye. There was reason for optimism for the health sector. Senior doctors like Sebastian Kyalwazi, J.C. Ssali, George Kamya, Edward Kigonya, Marcel Otim, Justus Byarugaba, and Jack Jaggwe who had hang on when everything seemed to be disintegrating, knew that their patience had not been in vain.

The new government brought unexpected prosperity to some. As Head of Department, a professor who had not driven a car in a decade got a brand new Suzuki. A few days after the arrival of the Suzuki, he drove into town to do some banking. He parked the car outside Grindlays Bank on Kampala Road and got into the bank. He came out some thirty minutes later, and instinctively, his feet led him down the path that he had walked regularly for the preceding several years. He crossed Kampala Road, walked down Luwum Street, and went down into the taxi park.

He got a taxi to Mulago in good time for his afternoon lecture. A few hours later he emerged from the department, and alas, the new Suzuki was nowhere in sight! Those days there were very few cars in the parking, so a quick look was enough to establish that the car was gone. An alarm was immediately raised, as it became apparent that someone had stolen the professor's new car. The case was reported at the Police Post down by the Casualty Department, and Police all across Kampala were alerted to be on the look-out for the car. The following morning, a Police officer came to the professor's office and informed him that a car fitting the exact description of his stolen car was parked outside Grindlays Bank, and it looked undisturbed. At the mention of Grindlays, the professor blinked a couple of times and reached for his well-used leather bag. Sure enough, the Suzuki keys were there. He thanked the police officer, and announced that the car had been recovered. Out of respect for grey hair, nobody asked how the car got where it was in the first place.

***

In the late 1980s the medical community was introduced to 'new' infections. Some were known and had in fact been common at one time in the distant past, but there were a few entirely new ones. They had names that young doctors had never heard of: *Cryptococcus neoformans, pneumocystis carinii, toxoplasmosis.* The only reason these rare organisms were able to re-emerge was because the Human Immunodeficiency Virus (HIV) had so weakened the patients' immune systems that almost anything could now take root and grow. The weak system was allowing them the opportunity to establish themselves, and to prosper where they otherwise would not have. That meant that in treatment it was not good enough just to kill the offending organisms, as others would very rapidly replace them. One had to find ways to boost the immunity of the patients to the point where their bodies would not give opportunity to the organisms to flourish. What made it very challenging was that the organs that ordinarily defended the body were themselves the first to come under attack. It was as though the enemy was coming in quietly, burning down the arsenals and armories around the country, and then going on the rampage. Even if the army knew that the enemy was present, even if they could see the enemy troops, they would have no means of countering the attacks. Treatment plans in these immunosuppressed patients were fire-fighting from frightening beginning to painful finish. Doctors were throwing antibiotics at this bug, anti-virals at that one, anti-fungals this week, and more antibiotics the following week. Finally, chemotherapy would be called in when an opportunistic cancer reared its ugly head. All this in a patient much weakened by disease, ravaged by constant fevers, and barely able to eat or keep any food down. The assault was usually relentless. The end was always predictable.

What was not predictable, and what warmed the heart in those dark and seemingly endless months and years of losing patients almost as fast as they came in, was the fighting spirit of the medical staff. They might be exhausted, they might be poorly paid, some might be sick themselves, but they never gave up the fight. The nurses fetched the medicines from the pharmacy and handed them out to bony hands wrapped in dry spotted skin. But they handed them out anyway. They put up intravenous lines on patients that they knew were going to be dead the following day. But they still put the lines up anyway. The doctors did rounds, examined patients whose diagnoses were obvious even to the illiterate relatives, and they ordered for tests and sent off specimens – they did what they knew best to do, day after wretched day.

Dr. Elly Katabira, a young physician who had just returned from the UK, set up a clinic to treat patients with HIV and the resulting Acquired Immunosuppressive Disease Syndrome (AIDS). The clinic was almost instantly the most crowded clinic in the hospital. He and his team were working from 7 am until the last patient was seen, usually late in the afternoon. He came under criticism from even his close colleagues, who argued that the hospital needed to create a special ward for those affected by this new killer, and not to be seeing all those patients in the same space used by other clinics. His counter argument was that nobody knew how long the hospital was going to ride the tide. What proportion of the population was affected? What would they do when more and more patients came? Create more special wards? Where would they get the staff to work in the special ward? It was early days, he argued – the medical profession did not know enough about how the disease was being transmitted, so everyone had to be on high alert. Precautions had to be taken by everyone all the time, in every patient encounter.

While the debate was still raging, patients started turning up in every ward and discipline, with symptoms suggestive of HIV. Pregnant mothers. Young men with charcoal-black wounds on the soles of their feet that would not heal. Small children with unusually aggressive jaw tumors. Talk of creating a special ward died a natural death. The medical fraternity, irrespective of ward or department, rolled up their sleeves and went to work. They started to notice patterns and pointers. Like a team of detectives, they carefully documented every clue, and filed it away as the evidence against the new virus mounted. It was many of those observations, made by ordinary doctors, nurses, radiographers, and pathologists, that made significant contributions to the fight against HIV. For doctors such as Elly Katabira, David Serwadda, and Nelson Sewankambo, the study of the virus and its effects on patients, their families and communities, came to define lifetime careers.

It soon emerged that HIV not only could, but was in all likelihood being transmitted through blood and other body fluids. For the medical staff this was very frightening. It struck terror in every heart. Medical workers had been handling immunosuppressed patients with no protection whatsoever. Needles were being boiled for reuse. Gloves were being washed and reused in places like the operating rooms and maternity wards. Nobody had ever had reason to wear two pairs of gloves at the same time, a practice that soon became standard as awareness about the epidemic increased. It was common, especially during long operations and procedures involving splintered bone, for the surgeons to finish the operation, peel off their gloves, and find a bloody finger or thumb, an indication that there had been a leak in the glove. A bone splinter or a needle prick? Was that the patient's blood, or the surgeon's? Had the patient's blood found its way into the surgeon's bloodstream? That might happen even when one was aware that the patient they were operating carried the virus. With confirmed transmission through blood, one would have expected one of two things to happen: either that the hospitals would rapidly empty of health workers terrified of contracting HIV, or that the government would jump into action to ensure that there were enough resources to make precautions against HIV transmission not just available, but mandatory everywhere. Neither happened. Universal precautions, as they came to be known, became another one of those things that in a rational world should be taken for granted, but in Uganda they joined a long list of health care needs that were never met, because somehow, the money could not be found. There was always another financial year, sometime in the future. How many health workers contracted the virus through contact with patients, even after the modes of transmission had become clear, will never be known.

THE NUTTY NINETIES

Those who here be, Seek ye the truth
Build for the future, the great Makerere
Those here have been, Those here will be
Build for the future,
The Great Makerere

Benjamin Semakula started off intending to go to Mengo Hospital. But as he was leaving the house it occurred to him that he had never been to that hospital as a patient, and he did not really want to go there. He would go to Mulago. That was what made sense. Semakula had retired some 15 years back from Mulago Hospital, where he had been an anesthetic officer for more than thirty years. He had joined the staff as a theatre nurse during the time Prof. McAdam was Head of Surgery, and he had worked in his theatre. Because he was very handy, he was often asked to assist the anesthetist with cleaning the equipment and watching the patients in recovery room. Over time he was encouraged to train as an anesthetic assistant, and by the time Prof. Kyalwazi took over as Head of Surgery, he was working as an anesthetist. He knew every surgeon that ever practiced in the hospital, and most knew him as well.

He walked along the familiar corridor from the second floor parking, past the Radiology Department, and through the double doors of the Department of Surgery. The doors squeaked and groaned badly, partly because the right one was unhinged at the top. He stood just outside the department secretary's office, and noticed a long line-up of portraits to the right. He moved closer and realized they were portraits of all the heads of department since the creation of the department back in 1928.

A young lady looked up from a magazine. "*Wangi sebo?*" "Yes sir?"

"*Omukulu mwali?*" "Is the Head in?"

"*Nedda.*" "No"

She went on to explain that if he was a patient he should go to the Surgical Outpatient Clinic, as the Head of Department did not see patients in the office. She turned back to her magazine, making it clear that the conversation was over. Semakula could see the inner door that led to the office of the Head of Department. He had been in that office a few times to see Prof. Kyalwazi. When he needed a hernia operation Kyalwazi saw him from the ward, but for his follow-up he examined him here. He wondered if someone had changed the furniture. A heavy set mahogany desk at which Kyalwazi sat with his back to the window; an examination table in the corner, where he had been examined; a bookshelf directly opposite the desk, facing the window. Strange, he thought, that he should be standing outside this office, at a loss for what to do. He was now an unknown old man, probably seen as an inconvenience. He was about to move away when a young looking doctor came in through the squeaky double doors.

"Good morning Florence," he called.

"Morning Sir". The secretary did not lift her head from her magazine.

The doctor walked right by Semakula without so much as a glance, paused very briefly at the secretary's desk, then turned and entered the office of the Head of Surgery. Could he be the Head? He looked too young to be Head, but Semakula noted that he had entered the office with an air of confidence. The thought of appealing to the youthful doctor over his current health problems was unappealing. But maybe he could recommend one of his older colleagues. He approached the secretary again, and waited for her to take her attention from the magazine. After a long while, she got up and went to the tray by the edge of the table where a number of files were pending. She was being deliberate in not addressing him. It was not possible that she did not notice him waiting for her attention. Any other time he would have simply walked away, but the pain in his back was reminder enough that he really needed to see a doctor. He turned as though to go away, but something rose up in him, from somewhere deep in his chest, an anger, a refusal to be ignored. Without thinking about what he was going to say, he found himself walking to the inner door, and opening it without knocking. It happened so quickly, the secretary was caught off guard. She started to protest, rebuking him for the disruption. But that one act of defiance had called to the surface the old Semakula, the one that refused to be put down, the one that had risen from a dresser to a nurse, all the way up to anesthetist by sheer determination, probably before this secretary was born. He looked back once and firmly closed the door in her face. There!

***

The Accident and Emergency Department (A&E) was perhaps the busiest place in all of Mulago Hospital. It was loud and chaotic, but there was method to this madness. There was an ebb and flow, and patients were seen around the clock. It covered a wide area. The main entrance led into a hall of sorts where patients were registered and sorted, and where they might wait a few minutes or several hours to be seen by a health worker. Wide swing doors separated this area from the treatment and resuscitation rooms to the right. Further down the corridor past the treatment rooms was an X-ray unit, and operating rooms were at the extreme end. It was mostly in the space beyond the swing doors that patients were saved or lost. It was here that destinies were changed. Beyond the waiting room, going deeper into the hospital, was the Emergency Admission ward, also called 3B Emergency, or simply 3BE. In theory all patients that came to the A&E could stay only until 8.00 AM of the following day. At that point, the doctors who had been on call would do the rounds, and discharge those who were well enough to go home. The rest of the patients would go to the wards for longer hospitalization. From around 9.00am when the rounds ended, the nurses and porters were busy transferring patients to various wards. But there were many patients that neither went home nor found beds in the already overcrowded wards.

In reality 3BE never emptied. Soon enough new patients would begin to arrive, and by afternoon the ward would be full again. Over the next 18 hours patients would continue to be admitted, occupying every conceivable space until it was not possible to move between beds without stepping over a patient. On particularly busy days, sick children shared beds, and there were patients under the beds and in the corridors. In these conditions, few bedside procedures were possible, and indeed many were simply not done. The two nurses on duty had to be experts at determining how to apportion their most precious resource – their time. Doctors would by habit write instructions like 'monitor blood pressure every 2 hours', or 'keep a fluid input-output chart', but both the doctors and nurses knew that nothing of the sort was going to happen. It had been years since such charts were routine. The hospital did not even print the required stationery anymore. And if they had, there was no chance that they would be used. If a nurse on duty started recording the patients' vital signs in such charts as required by either the doctor or the patient's condition, he would never do anything else. The same nurse needed to admit patients, go to the pharmacy to fetch drugs and supplies, hand out medicines, and assist the doctor to do some emergency procedures. He then needed to write a report and hand over to the next shift when the time came.

Sometimes the nurse would see a patient once – when the patient first came to the ward. All of those instructions that the doctor wrote concerning the patient would go unattended, because by the time the doctor made their way through the sea of patients, taking histories, examining patients, writing prescriptions and the endless unheeded instructions, the nurse would have to move on to other equally urgent duties. Some patients needed to be prepared for emergency operations. Some were just being wheeled back from the operating room, with tubes and bottles that needed attention. These critically ill patients were usually kept close to the nurses' desk so that they could keep an eye on them, with the help of their relatives. Here the relatives – also euphemistically called attendants – were the real nurses. They fed their patients, cleaned them, gave them their medicines, and in some cases they even changed their dressings. It mattered not that most of these relatives had until now never held a bandage in their hands, and that they had no understanding of the world of microbes and antiseptics, the overstretched nurses fully expected them to change soiled dressings, and to feed unconscious patients through tubes that run through the nose into the stomach.

***

The Post-graduate students' common room, or PG room as it was known, was a second home to the Senior House Officers, who spent more time there than they did in their homes. When not in the hospital, chances were they were here, reading, napping, discussing cases, arguing, and drinking endless cups of tea. Subjects ranged from patient care – theater flooded again, so no operations today, the patient run away, that patient that looked half dead is walking about today, I don't believe that biopsy result, I think I will send for a repeat, if I don't get an ICU bed for that kid now she is going to succumb, I suspect my samples were subjected to the sink test .., to sports, to girls and guys, to religion, to politics – any and everything could be discussed here. If a resident was worried about an operation they were planning, they could recruit an assistant among the group, so that the risk was shared. Or someone would offer a suggestion if they had done a similar case before. If a patient died and one was feeling awful, this was the place to come and bare one's heart – people understood. Everyone here had lost a patient that they set out to save. Everyone had missed a diagnosis. There was usually no judgment here, only understanding and a certain kind of sibling support. There were some fights, but never nasty ones. There was an awareness that the surgery residency was not a party, but a stormy sea of sorts, and that while everyone had their own individual destiny, for now they needed to row together if they were going to survive.

The topic of the month was not a surgical problem, but a surgeon. On 18 November 1994 a female general surgeon, Specioza Wandira Kazibwe, made history by being appointed Vice President.

"Maybe she will remember where she came from, and surgeons will be paid better," someone started.

"Are you kidding? There is no shortage of doctors in Cabinet. None of them has remembered where they came from, if by that you mean they will lobby for higher salaries for their medical colleagues."

Kazibwe would defy all odds, and serve as Vice President for a record eight years. The media probably mistook her for a naïve token female that would be best advised to keep her mouth pretty and smiling but safely shut. She gave them one scandalous sound-bite after another, ranging from saying the male MPs needed to wash their socks, to advocating for the sexual rights of animals. But Kazibwe proved to be no push over, as she managed to survive the political roller coaster that was being Museveni's Vice, for nearly a decade. Her exit was as flowery as her tenure.

***

Karungi came out of the PG room and, turning the corner a little too fast, almost ran into a small bodied woman that was lugging a big bag behind her. She excused herself and stepped aside to let the woman pass, and was hurrying away when she heard the woman call after her. "Rungi!"

Karungi span around, her heart skipping a beat. She was instantly thrown some 20 years back. Only one person in the world ever called her that.

"Biitu!"

"Yes!" The small woman dropped her bag and came forward hesitantly. Karungi run forward, and threw her arms around the spare frame, almost knocking her off the ground. The two women hugged and laughed and hugged some more. Then Karungi held Biitu by the shoulders and moved back a step to take a good look at her childhood friend.

"Where have you been? What have you been up to? What are you doing here? How did you find me? …"

"Hey … slow down! Let me explain."

"Okay, let us get out of the cold and mosquitoes." Karungi opened the PG room and switched on the lights. She pulled a lab stool for her friend, and perched herself on a chair opposite her.

"So – tell me …"

Biitu took a deep breath and started. She and her husband had moved to Nyabushozi where he worked at a cattle ranch. Biitu's father had passed on, and the rest of the family had relocated to a more remote village in a neighboring district. Her husband had died two years back, leaving her with their five children, the oldest now sixteen, and the youngest six. A year after the husband died Biitu started having irregular vaginal bleeding and pain in the lower abdomen. Several hospital visits and unsuccessful treatments later, it was discovered that she had cancer of the cervix. The doctor who broke the news told her the cancer was fairly advanced, but he said that radiotherapy would help. So here she was trying to get an appointment at the Radiotherapy Unit.

"So who is watching the kids while you are here?"

"Our first boy Koojo is old enough. We have a stall in the market where he sells porridge. Lydia, my oldest girl, helps him with the cooking after school. They are alright."

Karungi could remember when they were twelve. They could not possibly have made meals for the family. But this was the era of child-led households. Here were two kids holding the fort while their mother traveled to Kampala to receive radiotherapy for a potentially fatal condition.

Biitu had changed a great deal with the years. She wore a bulky weave that framed her small face, giving her more body. Bushy untamed eyebrows hang over quick brown eyes. Her colorful African print dress was fitting down to the waist, and opened into a full skirt, giving her a girly appearance. She waved her strong, well-worked hands as she recounted her story.

The one thing that had not changed despite five children, the death of a husband, and a cancer diagnosis, was Biitu's mischievous grin and infectious optimism. Looking at her face, one would have thought that she was here over some trivial complaint. It was amazing how, in a country as small as Uganda, the two close childhood friends had not seen each other in decades. Karungi had completed secondary school and gone on to medical school, then internship, and now a residency in surgery. No husband, no kids. Their worlds could not have been more different.

The two women would have carried on talking, but just then Karungi's pager went off. She jumped up, took a look at it, and grabbed her clinical coat. "Let's talk as we walk. I am on call and will be heading to theatre shortly," Karungi told her friend.

At the rail, she pointed Biitu to the footpath that led to the Radiotherapy hostel, and dashed down to the A&E. She would look in on her in the morning.

***

Patients started arriving at the Radiotherapy unit as early as 6.30am. Usually the nurses and doctors would begin to arrive around 8.00am, and the treatments would begin shortly after that. But this morning was unusual. After hours of waiting, the patients were told that a crucial piece of the radiotherapy machine was not working, and that the replacement would have to come from Europe. All the patients were advised to go home and return after a couple of weeks.

Biitu did not think she would be able to turn around that quickly. Maybe after a couple of months. Before she left to go back to the village, Biitu talked about how wonderful it would be to get some good amount of porridge flour. They would be able to raise next term's fees from it. Biitu might be gone by then, but she was confident that the son would manage. She talked about her impending death almost as though she was going to some foreign country from which she would return at some future date. Karungi helped her to get the flour, and she was beside herself with gratitude. Apart from the hefty bag containing maize flour and other groceries, Biitu had a roomy handbag that carried two bottles of oral morphine, a type of strong pain relief medicine given to patients with painful terminal conditions. Karungi drove her to the bus park in downtown Kampala and waited until all of her bags had been put in the hold. Biitu found a nice seat by the window and waved happily to Karungi, who waved back before driving off amidst impatient honks from drivers waiting to take the parking spot. The thought crossed her mind that she might not be seeing her childhood friend again, ever.

***

Kweete had been in the Heart Institute enough times that many of the nurses there knew her by name. When Karungi came in Kweete had an oxygen mask over her face, with a tube running from a cylinder by the side of the bed. There was a meter on this cylinder to show how much oxygen was being delivered. She recalled a time when she was in this same ward, maybe same cylinder, and instead of the oxygen meter there was a disposable water bottle with flimsy rubber tubes stuck through its cover. Things were looking up. What caught her attention though, were Kweete's nails. They were perfectly polished a gleaming crimson red. She wondered who had been here painting the nails of a woman so sick that she needed an oxygen mask.

The Mulago Hospital where Kweete lay was opened a week after Uganda got its independence from colonial master Britain. But a more modest facility had occupied the upper part of the hill that bore the same name for nearly half a century. That older facility came to be known as Old Mulago, and its younger sibling as New Mulago. Though decades separated their births, the two were like Siamese twins, intimately connected, their fates intricately linked, sharing not just the last name, but water and power supply lines, staff, and the steady stream of patients that went between the two.

At the time of its opening, New Mulago was one of the best hospitals on the African continent. The thirteen operating theatres had piped oxygen and suction, and the lights had cameras for televising operations. Sterilization was by high-speed automatic autoclaves. To reduce on the noise within the hospital, the architect had used open corridors and large ventilating spaces which created "islands of accommodation surrounded by a sea of breeze". Each ward had 54 beds and a side-room where simple pathological investigations could be done, and where students could be taught. The laundry was wholly mechanized, and included a foul-wash area and a central linen bank. The mortuary had four postmortem tables, body refrigeration, offices, changing-rooms with showers for staff and students, two viewing-rooms, and a large lecture-demonstration theatre. It was mechanically ventilated and has ultraviolet lamps on the ceiling.[11] The staff were trained to the highest standard available anywhere in the world. "Throughout the course, standards obtaining in the best British medical schools apply. External examiners from Britain take part in the professional examinations. It is quite exceptional for a student who enters the medical course not to qualify."[12]

That was back in the 1960s. By the time the millennium rolled along, all evidence of piped oxygen and suction had vanished, and water shortages were not infrequent. Decades of neglect had erased all vestiges of the pristine and efficient environment that had been the hallmark of Mulago Hospital. Yet there were small pockets both in the hospital and Medical School complex that were thriving.

---

[11] A. Alderdice, M.B. Sydney. The New Mulago Hospital. *Lancet* 3 August 1963: 237-240
[12] J. A. Tulloch, M.C., M.D. Edin., M.R.C.P., F.R.C.P.E., Professor of Medicine and Former Dean of the Medical Faculty. The Faculty of Makerere University College. In: *Lancet* 3 August 1963: Page 240

The doctors ordered for tests of Kweete's blood. Karungi opted to take her cousin's samples to the TB research lab for the tests. It was located on the topmost floor of the decrepit Pathology Building, but it had state-of-the-art equipment from the USA. To get to it one walked along dusty ground floor corridors and past smelly toilets, with cobweb vines from long dead weavers still swinging in the corners, and up four flights of chipped terrazzo stairs until the final landing. On the extreme left was a steel door with an ultra-modern sensor at eye level. Paul who headed the lab, and who Karungi had appealed to for help, placed his index finger over the sensor and the door slid silently open. It closed behind them ever so gently, that Karungi barely noticed. The room was air conditioned, and spotless clean – maybe even sterile. It was a long lab extending easily the length of a good 20 meters. There were refrigerators along the wall on one side, and several pieces of equipment at workstations on the other side. Lab technicians in white coats were busy. And quiet. Paul asked Karungi when the samples were submitted, and walked to the desk in one corner where the records were kept. He punched the information into a console, and after a brief interval there was the gentle purr of a printer, and the results rolled out. Paul explained that any specimens whose results were contentious after being reviewed by two specialists were sent digitally to two different reference labs – one in India, and one in Ohio, USA. Within twenty four hours they usually had two expert opinions with which to compare their own results. Armed with these latest results, Karungi hurried back to the Heart Institute where Kweete's doctors would determine the most suitable medication.

***

Winnie came from the ward to find a young man waiting outside PG room. He asked if Dr. Ogundi was around. "I don't know." Winnie tried the door and found it locked. "Clearly not. Do you have an appointment?"

"No, but he operated my mother, and she is now well and has been discharged. I thought I would see him before we leave the hospital.

The Patient

I will wait." Winnie entered the room and forgot about him until a couple of hours later when she came out to find him still waiting outside.

"Maybe you should try the ward. Or leave him a message," she suggested. The young man said he had been to the ward and had not found him. Winnie turned round and swung the door wide open. "There – that is his desk." The young man reached into the big *kikapu* – a bag woven out of palm leaves – and pulled out a black plastic bag. She could see the head of a live chicken peeping through a hole in the bag. She was about to say he could not leave the chicken there but thought it might be an interesting surprise for Ogundi. 'Sure, put it over there in the corner." He did, Winnie banged the door shut and headed off to the A&E.

Ntege and Francis came back and opened the door. Ntege sat at his desk while Francis went to the board and started working on a new sketch. Suddenly a rustling sound broke out from under the table. They both turned to look. Silence. A minute or so later there was another sound, then right before their eyes, a hefty black plastic bag emerged from under the table, and as though propelled by some unseen hand, started to make its way across the floor in the direction of the board. It quacked and clicked, and lurched forward in a zigzag manner, getting closer to Francis with every move. The usually calm Ntege bolted from his corner and was out of the door in a flash, all the while yelling, "*askari!*" "Guard!" Francis leapt into the air and attempted to land on top of one of the desks. He narrowly missed, and landed with one foot on a chair, while the other foot slid off the top of the desk and flew into the air. He came crashing down to the floor, with his head now only a few inches from the mysterious black bag, which was now quacking more loudly. A guard came running, almost rammed into Ntege, and asked him what the matter was. From the doorway, Ntege pointed to the bag. By this time though, the chicken's head had found its way out of the hole, and was now in full view. "You doctors are afraid of a chicken?" He laughed with relief and walked away. Neither of the doctors thought it was funny.

After that incident, it was agreed that nobody would accept packages of any sort on behalf of a colleague.

***

On 11 March 1996 Mutyaba was in a taxi heading to Mulago when he heard over the radio that a *mzungu* had been shot and killed in Mulago during a car robbery. The *mzungu*'s name was Belcher. Mutyaba was devastated. It was a Monday, and he had worked with Belcher on the Friday before. They still had plans for the expansion of the orthopedic program. Belcher had been very much alive and full of ideas. He had confided in Mutyaba that NATO was decommissioning some hospitals, and they might be getting a helicopter ambulance from that. The two of them had discussed the potential value of such a service. Belcher had not been just a resourceful individual and an outstanding surgeon. He had been a mentor, a colleague, and a friend.

***

> Address to the United States Senate by Senator Patrick Joseph Leahy (Vermont). Congressional Record, United States Senate, 13 March 1996:
>
> Mr. President, it is with great sadness that I rise today to inform the Senate of the tragic death of Dr. Rodney Belcher, an orthopedic surgeon from Arlington, VA, who was murdered in Kampala, Uganda, on March 11 [1996]. I was fortunate to have known Dr. Belcher.

The Patient

Seven years ago, shortly after I established the War Victims Fund, a $5 million appropriation in the foreign aid program to provide medical and related assistance to war victims, Rod Belcher signed on with Health Volunteers Overseas. He had lived in Uganda before the civil war there, and the Agency for International Development sent him back to start a War Victims Fund program to assist people who had been disabled from war injuries. He and his wife Dawn had been there ever since. There were tens of thousands of amputees, many victims of landmines, without access to artificial limbs. The Mulago hospital and medical school, once the pride and joy of that country, were in ruins. There were not even basic medical supplies. There was not a single trained orthopedic surgeon in the country. The Ugandan Government was bankrupt. Rod embraced that enormous challenge with enthusiasm, good humor, patience, and a deep, personal commitment to the Ugandan people. Over the years, he won the trust and respect of the Ugandan Government, and of successive United States Ambassadors and the ambassadors of other countries who witnessed the impact he was having on the lives of so many people. He rebuilt the orthopedic clinic and trained every orthopedic surgeon in Uganda today. He had a warmth and gentleness, and a commitment to Uganda that was extraordinary. Mr. President, on March 13, on his way to his office, Dr. Belcher was murdered when two men stole his car. He was shot in the chest and died right there. It would be hard to conceive of a more senseless, horrible crime. Rod Belcher was a wonderfully generous human being who devoted his professional life to improving the lives of others. For the past 7 years he lived and worked in a country where getting even the simplest thing accomplished often required incredible ingenuity and persistence. Rod had both. At his funeral, Dr. Belcher was honored by the Ugandan Vice President, the Minister of Health, the director of the hospital, the dean of the medical school, the American Ambassador, the British High Commissioner, and many others. The orthopedic clinic that he worked so hard to establish was formally named after him.

> The streets were lined with people who knew him personally or had heard of the American doctor who had done so much for the Ugandan people. Rod Belcher will be terribly missed. But he leaves a legacy that anyone would be proud of. He gave the War Victims Fund its start, and for that, I will always be grateful. He leaves a core of trained Ugandan orthopedic surgeons who loved and admired him, who will carry on in his place.

***

Karungi was preparing to go to lunch after a relatively quiet morning when she heard the sound of the Police Patrol vehicle in a distance. She had come to know when it was the one. In a few minutes the truck pulled up outside the A&E, and a couple of policemen jumped out of the cabin. They started to offload their cargo. The Uganda Red Cross volunteers materialized and helped the policemen to extract what looked like critically ill patients from under the seats in the back of the truck. There was a young man and two kids. One of the kids was wailing and calling for the mother. The other was ominously quiet. The young man's shirt was hanging in shreds and covered in mud. The team got busy with the trio, and they were finishing up when a medical records clerk came to announce that there was another patient with head injury.

***

The patient came in with a slowly expanding blood clot over the right side of his brain. The history and signs were typical. The 35 year-old man had been thrown off a *boda-boda* when it collided with a pick-up truck. He fell into a ditch and was badly shaken, but seemed to be fine shortly afterwards. Over the next few hours he became confused, incoherent, and finally slipped into unconsciousness. Clearly, he was continuing to bleed, and the resulting blood clot was putting pressure on the brain. A surgical procedure was needed to remove the clot, and time was of the essence. The surgeon was ready, the patient was ready, and the operating room was alerted. There was one problem. The operating room did not have the necessary equipment and supplies. Some, like wax and sutures (threads used in surgical operations), were easy enough to find in a pharmacy, although their quality might be questionable. But others, such as diathermy – a tool that works much like a welding gun, except in this case it cauterizes and instantly seals the tiny blood vessels that cause problematic bleeding during surgery – one did not just go out and buy. Dr. Senyonyi swore that he was not going to, as he put it, "kill another patient in the name of an emergency operation".

The family got wind of it. They thought this was an excuse by the medical staff to extract money from the desperate relatives. One of the older women approached the nurse and asked if she could speak to the doctor. The doctor came out. The lady asked the doctor if they needed money to buy anything for the surgery – a polite way of asking if they should organize an inducement. "No," the doctor said. He explained about the equipment.

"So what do we do?"

"I don't know." The lady did not move. The doctor started to walk away. He felt trapped. In a couple of hours he was going home, and without the operation the patient would be gone when he got back the following day. It was one thing to lose a patient who had a rapidly growing malignant tumor in his brain; it was another to lose one that could be saved by such a straightforward procedure – if one had the right equipment. He turned back to the lady.

"They have the equipment at Nakasero Hospital."

"How much does it cost?" Despite the gravity of the problem the doctor chuckled. He had known patients to suggest that they buy all manner of equipment. A high ranking soldier once asked him how much it cost to buy an operating microscope. These were not things one bought from a corner drug shop.

"I don't know how much it costs, but you don't have time to go and import it. You would need to transfer the patient there."

"How much does it cost to have him operated from there then? And do we have to find another surgeon, or do you work there as well?"

"I don't know what it costs, and no, I do not work there. But if you want to move him you do not have much time. If the pressure over his brain is not relieved soon the part of his brain that controls his heart and breathing will die …" He let the word 'die' hang in the air. "…*will die* …"

The lady moved back to the small group huddled at the bottom of the patient's bed. She recounted the exchange with the doctor. A heated discussion followed. There were consultations on phones. After a while the lady that had initiated the discussion approached the doctor's office again. "Doctor, we want to go. Please give us the referral."

Dr. Senyonyi had long stopped worrying about these so-called reverse referrals. Mulago was the national referral hospital, and in principle, the most advanced medical institution in the country. In theory, one could not go higher, or get better care than that. The doctors had been instructed to not send patients to lower level hospitals except for follow-up. Those instructions were useless in the face of the current shortages. Many smaller hospitals in the city were better equipped, and it was no secret that patients were often moved from Mulago to smaller facilities for better care. And it was not just for the equipment. Some Mulago Hospital specialists had not stepped in the hospital's operating rooms for years. One consultant specialist had referred to Mulago, only half in jest, as a fishing pond. The patients came to the pond, and the doctors came to fish for the ones that could afford better services at other hospitals. Those that remained in Mulago could not afford better facilities.

***

Josephine Nabulime walked into the Accident & Emergency Department a few minutes to 8.00am as she had done countless times before. She was a near permanent fixture in the ward, moving in and out of the treatment cubicles, but spending most of her time in the main resuscitation room. The most critically ill patients were brought here, usually for life saving procedures – blocked airways were cleared, and artificial airways were inserted. Intravenous drips were set up, and if a patient needed an emergency operation the operating room was only meters away. Nabulime knew every inch of this room, and she treated the equipment here like her prized personal possessions. She had been praying for a ventilator – even a used one – but that had not happened yet. Today was going to be difficult though. There had been no oxygen the previous night, and she had heard on her way in that the situation had not changed. The nurse in charge of pediatric Acute Care Unit had told her that the unit lost four babies in as many hours after the oxygen run out. 'We had four babies sharing an oxygen cylinder, and the room had two cylinders. When the first cylinder run out we tried to move the babies onto the remaining one. It was a stretch, fitting all eight babies on one cylinder. Then around nine in the night the second cylinder run out as well. I was just leaving. I left the night duty nurses running all over the place to try and find some oxygen.'

Nabulime went to the little cubicle where the nurses kept their street shoes and changed into the more comfortable pair that she wore at work. She then went to the office of the A&E In-charge, where she usually reported to see if there were any particular instructions for the day. The office was locked. She went through the cubicles, and was relieved that they were all empty. The trolleys and floor still had evidence of the night's emergencies – the sharps containers were full, there were abandoned blood stained sandals on a trolley, and a half empty bottle of saline hang over one of the beds, with the catheter sticking out. Josephine had had many conversations with the nurses on the night shift about the state of these rooms. If they were not cleaned as soon as patients were moved, there was always the chance that another patient could come in dire need of stabilization, and the confusion that was generated by trying to clean the cubicles as new patients waited increased chances of cross infection. She was considering going off to complain to the nurse in charge of the cubicles when she spotted a Police patrol vehicle make the curve from the fourth level heading towards the A&E entrance on the third level. "Here we go," she said under her breath.

Nabulime ran back into the cubicles, pulled a pair of gloves on, and quickly started to clean up. She wiped all accessible surfaces, and pulled down the offending saline bottle and dropped it into the bin. Then she hurried to the triage area to find two Red Cross volunteers wheeling a trolley towards the entrance, where two of their colleagues waited to move a patient from the back of the Police patrol pick-up truck onto the trolley. The pick-up trucks were the standard way patients were delivered to hospital following road traffic crashes or incidents involving violence. It was usually uncertain if the patients had been assaulted by the Police themselves or if they had sustained the injuries some other way. The Police were known to be quite brutal especially with demonstrators. The patient was pulled off the pick-up and onto the trolley. He was groaning, his face bloody and swollen. One of his legs was dangling at an awkward angle, prompting the Red Cross volunteers to slip a splint under it. There was no nurse at the triage desk so the patient was wheeled directly into the resuscitation area.

Nabulime quickly set about assessing the patient, and determining what needed to be done right away. An intern doctor came in just then, and the two continued the patient assessment and stabilization. She prayed that the oxygen would be delivered before it was needed. This was just the first of many patients, and eight hours later when her shift ended the unit still had no oxygen. She went by the surgical emergency ward to find the first patient lying on his back with a chest tube in place. The left side of his face looked even more swollen and was turning black, his left eye was not visible, and his breathing was regular but noisy. A heavy-set middle-aged woman sat on the floor by his bed. Josephine asked her how he was doing. "He has not woken up. They say he needs a special X-ray for his head but the machine to take the X-ray is not working. So we have been told he needs to be taken to another hospital for that. It will cost two hundred thousand shillings at that other hospital. We don't have it. I have sent for my husband. I think he will be here tomorrow."

Nabulime was familiar with this scenario. Some patients with head injury could not have surgery unless a special brain scan – CT scan – had been done, and the surgeons often insisted that patients stay in Surgical Emergency (Ward 3BE) ward until the scan could be done. Mulago's CT scanner was down more often than it was up and functioning, which meant that very ill patients were often bundled into an ambulance or some other form of transportation, and driven to one of Kampala's private facilities where the CT scan could be done. There was a different fate for patients whose relatives could not afford the scans.

****

Distressing working conditions had driven many health workers out of their chosen professions. KK remembered a young man she met in the mall a few years back. The young man had a stall selling curtains. Someone mentioned that he was a doctor. She thought it was a joke. It turned out to be true. She asked him why he chose curtains over the noble profession. "It stopped being noble," he said. He recounted how, during his internship, he had lost three babies in the same night because the Acute Care Unit had run out of oxygen. "I certified three deaths in one night. All three could have survived if we had had oxygen." "Oxygen!" he repeated, throwing his hands in the air. "The mothers kept pleading for my help. I run to the Director's office and found it locked. I run to the main theatre, not quite knowing what I expected from there. The anesthetist told me they had only enough oxygen for emergency operations, and he had two caesarean sections lined up. I went back to the ward to find the third baby gasping. The mother was wailing. I left the ward and did not go back until the following day. By that time I had made up my mind to either leave the country or the profession."

KK herself remembered many distressing nights during which she swore to leave Medicine altogether, but she always came back. One night when an operation had to be postponed for lack of oxygen, the patient's father asked her where they got the oxygen. "A factory delivers it."

"Yes, but where does the factory get it from? Do they import it or they manufacture it here?"

"No. Oxygen is actually in the air we breathe, but they use special equipment to extract it and pack it in the metallic drums that you see here."

The old man had kept quiet for a short while before wondering aloud. "If it is from the air it means Uganda cannot run out of oxygen. There is always enough in the air for all of us. How is it that a big hospital such as this one does not have the machine to catch it and pack it?"

***

THE MUCKY MILLENNIUM

'The present situation is appalling, not only because of the human misery that is the measure of the crisis, but also, and perhaps more importantly, because the group has lost the will to deal with the future at all. Everywhere the focus has shifted from the strategic responses which seek to lay foundations for the future … as the best leadership is sucked into equations of short term survival. The best minds no longer prepare for the tasks of the future, but are engulfed in the problems of the present.' Michael Manley, 1925 – 1997, on *'The rocky road to a new economic order'*

On Independence Day 2000, while most civil servants stayed home to enjoy the public holiday, a small band of public health specialists made their way to Gulu in northern Uganda on an urgent mission. The issue was one that would see the demise of hundreds of people before it burnt itself out. Ugandans were about to be introduced to the latest reason for the country's notoriety.

A couple living some 14 km north of Gulu town had died a mysterious death. The neighbors chalked it up to witchcraft, and all would have been settled, had another man that had attended the same funeral as the deceased couple not died a short while later in a similar manner. Acute fever, headache, vomiting blood, and bleeding from the gums. The new community diagnosis was food poisoning at the funeral. A few more people that had not been to the funeral fell ill with the same symptoms. Some were bleeding from not just the gums but the nose and eyes as well. They were taken to Lacor Hospital. Two of them died shortly after admission. Not too long afterwards, a couple of nurses that had taken care of the patients with the mysterious disease came down with the same symptoms. Now, that was alarming. The head of the hospital, Dr. Matthew Lukwiya, was away attending a course in Kampala, and he hastily returned to Gulu. He quickly recognized that this was a hemorrhagic fever epidemic from a highly contagious agent, very likely a virus. The race against time had just begun.

An urgent call was made to the Ministry of Health in Kampala on 8 October 2000, and the World Health Organisation (WHO) in Geneva was informed. A team of experts comprising of Ministry of Health staff, and experts from the WHO and Centers for Disease Control in USA, was dispatched the following day to assess the situation and collect samples for analysis. Blood samples were couriered to South Africa's National Institute of Virology in Johannesburg. A few days later, the results were back: *Ebola*. Once again the Ugandan health workers, having been informed of the highly contagious and rapidly fatal nature of the disease, rolled up their sleeves, draped and gloved as required, and went to work. Over the next several months, more than four hundred Ebola patients would be treated, and 224 of them would die.

In the fifth week of the epidemic Lukwiya woke up with a strange feeling all over his body. His muscles ached in a way they had not done before. He had been working long hours and having little sleep, so he thought this might explain his fatigue. He dragged himself out of bed and got ready for work. By mid-morning he was feeling so tired that he decided to go back home and catch up on some much needed sleep. He thought he might be coming down with the flu, or maybe malaria. The fever could not have picked a worse time. Lukwiya was managing a near-riot among the health workers who were terrified of contracting Ebola, and who thought the shifts were too long and the pay not commensurate with the risk. He had had to lead by example, doing rounds in the isolation ward daily. On the morning of the 27th November, as he got up from his bed, he felt a sudden wave of nausea. His heartbeat raced, and he felt a light-headedness that left him weak-kneed. All this lasted a minute or so; his head cleared, and his head stopped pounding. A nagging thought that had occurred to him earlier became more insistent, and took on a sinister name. Two of his nurses were in Intensive Care Unit fighting for their lives, so Lukwiya was well aware that the Ebola risk to health workers was very real. He had taken every precaution that he knew how, and he could not recall any incident that had exposed him to undue risk. Yet the symptoms that he was experiencing were unmistakable. He let Sr. Maria and his senior colleagues know about his suspicions, and a blood sample was taken. It returned positive for Ebola. He was taken into isolation ward. On 5th December Matthew Lukwiya lost the battle against the virus[13], leaving behind a team that was badly shaken by his death – some had been his students, most had worked with him closely as colleagues, and many were personal friends.

On 27 February 2001, five agonizing months after the epidemic started, Uganda was declared Ebola free.[14, 15, 16] It would be another seven years before a similar epidemic broke out, this time in Bundibugyo, a district well south of Gulu.

***

> Karungi arrived at the hospital just before 8.00 am, and headed straight to the Accident & Emergency Department. She had been on call the night before, and although it had been quiet, the admission ward round always took a while with new interns. The new batch was only a week into their surgical rotation. There was the usual patient mix. Burns, fractures and head injuries from *boda-bodas*, an intestinal obstruction, and old men with enlarged prostates. With all the decisions made and the patient transfers underway, Karungi went down to the Department of Surgery.

---

[13] Zurah Nakabugo & Simon Rasmussen. Dr Lukwiya's wife narrates how her husband contracted Ebola and died. *The Observer*. 4 October 2018.

[14] Samuel Ikwaras Okware 2015. Three Ebola outbreaks in Uganda. 2000-2011. Dissertation for the degree philosophiae doctor (PhD) at the University of Bergen, Norway.

[15] Outbreak of Ebola haemorrhagic fever in Uganda. European Center for disease Prevention and Control, Stockholm, Sweden. August 2012

[16] F G Omaswa, I Okware, E Kiguli-Malwadde. 2015. Strategies from the 2000–01 Ebola outbreak in Uganda. African Center for Global Health and Social Transformation, Kampala, Uganda. https://www.researchgate.net/publication/276899504_Strategies_from_the_2000-01_Ebola_outbreak_in_Uganda retrieved 14 June 2019.

"Ms. Karungi, you have a guest." The department secretary called after her as she passed by her door.

"Who is it?"

"There was a young man asking for you. I found him here when I came in around 7.30am. He said he is not a patient. I think it might be a relative. He should be just outside the door."

Just then, a young man walked in. "There he is."

Karungi had no idea who the young man was. "Yes, how can I help you?"

In response, the young man reached into his breast pocket and pulled out a brown envelope. He handed it to Karungi without speaking. Karungi reached out for it and tore it open. She was used to patients handing her lab results, old prescriptions, or referral notes from doctors in upcountry hospitals, and so she was unprepared for what she found. At first, she did not fully comprehend what she was reading until she was half way down the single page, torn out of a child's exercise book.

'Dear Rungi,

I do not think I will see you again. I am sorry to ask you for help like this. I do not know anyone else who can help. My girl Lydia is very bright. She always comes first in class even when she misses school often because of my illness. I do not want her to stop here in the village school. In many ways she reminds me of you when we were younger. She is always reading books, just as you did. We do not have enough books for her here. So this is my prayer. Can you find her a bursary? Can you help her to finish school? I think if she can finish S4, maybe she can become a nurse. Maybe one day she can even become a doctor. I know you will try. But if you are not able to, at least I know you will have tried. Thank you. Thank you very much.

God bless you. Biitu.'

The words were all carefully formed in a large, almost childish handwriting, with the letters sitting neatly on the printed lines. There was no date on the note.

Karungi was barely able to read the note to the end. There was a lump in her throat, and tears were running down her cheeks unchecked. She knew without asking. The young man stood a respectable distance away, saying nothing. Karungi read the note a second and third time. Finally, she looked up at the young man. "We buried her last month. I found the letter in her bag when I was cleaning her room out a few days ago. She had often talked about you. I thought I would bring it."

***

The PG Room in the Department of Medicine was quiet. The screams of the women in labor could be heard filtering through the windows from the maternity ward on the fifth floor above. The occupants of PG room were busy preparing for their exams, spread over a couple of weeks and beginning in a few days.

"For all the mayhem that comes in its wake, the Ebola virus is really not a successful parasite," Namubiru broke the silence.

"Meaning?"

"It kills most of its hosts. Almost everyone who gets Ebola becomes severely ill soon after. They die having had very few opportunities to pass the virus on to new hosts. So it burns itself out. Compare this with HIV. There are no symptoms, sometimes for years. That is plenty of opportunity to pass on the virus. So in the short term Ebola wreaks havoc, but long term it often does not impact the country as much as HIV has. The enemy that attacks you head-on at the first encounter is less dangerous than the one who begins by befriending you.

"That is very simplistic. The mayhem, as you call it, is often possible because there has been a more insidious destructive force. And the period of intense havoc is often followed by a prolonged period of slow and uncertain recovery during which more destruction happens. The one feeds into the other. Neither enemy is better than the other."

***

It had been a long clinic day, and the following day was theater day. The list of patients to be prepared for operation was already up on the board in the Sister's office. Francis came to the ward to pick up his bag. He opened the door and was reaching up into the locker when he became aware that someone was standing in the doorway. He busied himself with his bag, slowly pulled off his clinical coat and hung it up, all the while hoping that whoever it was would go away. He did not feel like another patient encounter. Finally he turned around and made it clear that he was leaving. A thin anxious looking woman he did not recognize stood resolutely in his path.

"*Musawo!*," she started. "Doctor!"

"*Wangi nyabo?*" "Yes Ma'am?"

She moved closer, invading his personal space, and gently unfolded her right fist to reveal some crumpled notes, maybe some ten thousand shillings altogether. "*Ze zoka zetulina.*" "This is all we have," she said.

"What is it for?"

"For Lukwago's operation tomorrow. We have been told that the doctors in theater want some money before they work on his leg. Please help us!" Francis started to protest but the woman placed the money on the table and hurried away.

The Patient

Lukwago was a 16 year-old boy with a tumor in his right leg just below the knee. All indications were that while the tumor was malignant in character, the disease was still limited to his lower leg. The plan was to amputate the leg above the knee, and follow that with chemotherapy, which would mop up any cancer cells that might have somehow gone past the level of the amputation, although they were not detectable at admission.

Lukwago had been prepared for theater three times, and three times his operation had been canceled. The first time oxygen ran out before his turn for theater came. The Red Firm on whose ward he was admitted had theater scheduled on Thursdays, so any operations that were not done for whatever reason were usually deferred until the following Thursday. The second Thursday that Lukwago was on the operating list a leak was discovered in the theater plumbing as work was just beginning. Part of the floor was flooded with what looked and smelt like sewage, and the sterility of the theater was breached. That day all operations were canceled, the plumbers were called in, and after that the operating rooms were scrubbed and fumigated to restore sterility. The third time Lukwago was prepared all seemed destined to go well. The first two patients were done without incident, and he was the third patient on the list. Just before he was wheeled out of the ward there was a call from Accident & Emergency theatre that three emergencies were lined up and there was no anesthetist. Red Firm was requested to suspend their non-emergency list so that the anesthetist could go and help out. He did not return. Lukwago was yet again told the operation was to wait another week. All this flashed through Francis' mind as he saw the lean figure of Lukwago's mother disappear down the corridor, with her *busuuti*, the voluminous dress common in central Uganda, swishing back and forth. He hurried after her. He felt awful. Of course she was right to suspect that the doctors were deliberately delaying her son's operation. Francis knew there were health workers demanding for money to get patients onto theater lists. If they wanted to get a patient to pay for a service, for instance to ensure that he got on the operating list for the following day, the technical word was 'bleeding'. A patient with money was said to have a good heamoglobin level – that one could be 'bled'. If a patient was perceived to have little or no money they were said to be 'anemic'. That meant they could not be bled, or they could only be bled using a very small needle. Some health workers were merciless. Even if a patient looked like they could use help themselves, as long as they were desperate enough to get into the discussion, they could be relieved of whatever little they still had on them.

"*Nyabo*," he called out. "Madam". She stopped and turned around. Francis caught up with her. Before he could launch into all the explanations about the delayed operation, she spoke. The words seemed to tumble out one on top of the other. "Lukwago's father was here yesterday. He wanted to take the boy to a traditional healer. I refused. Lukwago himself did not want to leave the hospital. The father left, but said we are now on our own. If the boy dies I should not call him."

"Of course he will be alright," Francis declared. "We shall operate his leg tomorrow." But even as Francis said this he could remember many other times when he had given patients assurances, and had had to eat his own words. It had been three weeks since the boy came to the hospital. In that time, the tumor could be breaking through the thin barriers provided by the false capsule, and tumor cells could now be coursing through his blood, and lodging themselves in his lungs, his liver … his brain. In ideal circumstances, this tumor should have been dealt with as an emergency. In Mulago these considerations always seemed academic.

The following day Francis was in theater bright and early. The list was long but Lukwago was only the second patient on the list. The first patient, a child with a mass on his neck, was done and finished without incident. Francis wrote the operation notes in the surgeon's room, and was walking back to the OR to scrub for Lukwago when he overheard a conversation that stopped him in his tracks. The Sister in Charge of the OR was talking to someone over the phone. "Well, if he is running a fever then you bring the next patient on the list."

"What?" he asked, as he turned to face the Sister. "Who is running a fever?"

"They say the patient for amputation has been running a fever since last night. This morning it was 39°C. I have asked them to bring the next patient – the exploratory lap." She marched off without waiting for Francis' response, presumably to go and change the instrument sets. She was losing no time over a patient that was unfit for theater. The rest of the operations were done and finished early. Francis dreaded seeing Lukwago and his mother, but he knew he had to explain this most unfortunate cancelation. He needed to let them get over the acute disappointment though. He determined that the following morning would be a good time, when the fever was controlled, and when he could explain how dangerous it would have been to undertake the procedure in that condition.

***

Francis noticed Lukwago's bed was empty as soon as he entered the ward. The bed was at the far end, but one could see it from the entrance to the ward. He was alarmed. "God, please let him be down in the lab. Or in the X-ray department." He approached the empty bed. Even the beddings were gone. In the next bed was another young man who had been on the ward with his leg in traction for a few weeks following a fracture of the thighbone. The two boys had struck up a friendship and spent the time playing cards across the narrow space between their beds. Francis did not have to ask.

"*Musawo*, Lukwago is gone. They left in the night. They did not take the X-ray films though." The young man pointed to the large brown envelope that contained the films, which had come at a substantial cost to the family, and which doctors had insisted must be done before he could be operated. Francis thanked the boy and moved away slowly, holding the envelope, not knowing what else to say.

He had stayed away from Katanga all these months. He had not touched alcohol in nearly half a year. Now he suddenly knew what he was going to do as soon as he left work. He hated this place. He needed something to drown the accusing voices in his head. All those patients that he had let down. He dropped Lukwago's films on top of the cabinet in the Sister's office and headed for the Surgical Outpatient clinic where he knew a long line of patients was already waiting. The day was just beginning, but all he could think of now was a drink of *waragi* down in Katanga.

***

In May 2003 Specioza Kazibwe announced that she was resigning from her position as Vice President. There had been little warning for those outside her close circle, but commentators were quick to say she had been hanging on by the skin of her teeth, and that her domestic woes had made it untenable for her to remain in the high profile, high pressure office. The exuberant girl from Busoga had ran a tough race, and although it was doubtful that she ever really wielded power as the Number Two in the country, she had managed to leave a mark in areas such as food security and female empowerment. For a surgeon though, she seemed to have hung her surgical gloves, and never looked back to see what her colleagues were battling in the trenches.

Kazibwe's resignation invoked mixed feelings among the Senior House Officers.

"Wow! Spe has resigned!" Namubiru was reading the cover page of the New Vision.[17, 18] "It will be interesting to see what she does now. Quite a change, given how long she has been Vice President."

"You will need to read the whole story. She has negotiated a severance package of US$ 1.25 million to enable her pursue a doctorate degree at Harvard, while her constituents in Kigulu South can barely afford enough calories to stay on the right side of malnutrition."

---

[17] Felix Osike, Okello Jabweli. Kazibwe resigns. New Vision 22 May 2003, Page 1.
[18] Ssemujju Ibrahim Nganda. Kazibwe PhD costs taxpayers 2.5 billion. Weekly Observer, 21 October 2004.

The Patient

"Hey – hang on there! You are using a really broad brush here," Agaba interjected. "For starters, Kazibwe did not resign. Anyone with their eyes half open could see that she was given two choices: to resign, or get fired. She jumped two seconds before she was pushed. She was simply given a soft landing, and told to get out of town while she was at it. Harvard is a dignified way of getting her out of the way.

"Soft landing? Dignified? Sounds to me like a deep plunge – a million dollars plus deep. And exactly whose dignity are we talking about here? The rest of us are left holding the bill while she enjoys life in the leafy suburbs of Boston."

"A PhD is not exactly a vacation," Namubiru pointed out.

"Well, that is what we are being told. Who knows if the PhD will happen? And even if it should happen, who needs a former surgeon and former Vice President with a million-dollar-PhD?"[19]

***

Registered Nurse Florence Kakayi was quiet spoken and polite to a fault. She seemed to apologise for her very existence. Yet when it came to work, Kakayi was tenacious. She could put needles in the tiniest, most tortuous veins. She had the kind of unquestioning compliance to instructions that a military officer would envy; an asset in the A&E. As long as she was able to, Kakayi did what the doctor asked her to do. But on the day a trailer carrying fuel overturned and caught fire somewhere along Jinja Road, Kakayi was anything but focused. She dropped things, forgot things, and was unusually inattentive. In frustration, KK, the surgeon on duty, told her to apply for a transfer to the skin clinic if she wanted to file her nails in the middle of the morning. To her utter surprise, Kakayi burst into tears. That is when it occurred to KK that there must be something badly wrong with

---

[19] Kazibwe got a severance package that she said was offered to her by the President. It included a fully paid PhD scholarship at Harvard, and full scholarships for her three children to study at prestigious universities in Europe and USA. The cost was estimated at UGX2.5 billion (USD1.25 million).

her. She assigned an intern to complete the procedure that Kakayi had just started, and called Kakayi out to the Sister's Room. "What is going on?"

"Doctor, my child is sick."

"What is the matter?"

"She has been convulsing almost non-stop since yesterday. I brought her to the Acute Care Unit in the night, and they have been trying to control the fits with no success. They say she needs phenytoin. It is out of stock in the hospital, so I need to buy it." There was a pause. "I have no money." The sobs became louder. Just then, the Sister-in-Charge came in. "Sister, do we have any phenytoin in our stock?"

"Ha! We have not had phenytoin for a long time. Pharmacy now only dispenses it to Pediatrics and Anesthesia. Those are your best chances."

KK was keenly aware that the burns patients from the trailer crash were still coming in, she could see more commotion in the corridor, and could imagine the Triage area was extremely busy. But for now all she could think of was Kakayi's child convulsing away somewhere in the hospital with no effective medication. And here Kakayi was, trying to stay at work, with no plan for how to come by the drug that her child desperately needed. How was she supposed to look after this sea of strangers when her own child's life was hanging in the balance?

KK invited Kakayi to go with her to the Administration Block on the fourth floor. The two walked through the crowded waiting area, and noticed that the Red Cross ambulance was still backed up at the entrance, offloading more patients. The Deputy Director was not in the office. They run down the stairs to the second floor and half run to the Main Pharmacy. KK went through the entrance and waved in greeting to the dispensers, but did not give them the chance to stop her. They did not like non-pharmacy staff coming through. She was in luck. The Chief Pharmacist was in his office on the phone. The duo stood in the doorway. Presently he got off the phone and asked what they wanted. KK got straight to the point. Pointing to Kakayi, she explained. "Her child has been convulsing since last night.

They need phenytoin. We understand it is out of stock in Acute Care. I am hoping you have some on reserve."

"Aha! This is not how we manage our stock. If every time something runs out on the wards you doctors come to my office ..." KK was having none of that. "Do you know what sustained convulsions are doing to that child's brain? Do you care? How many times have you seen me walking here to ask for medicines? This nurse is putting her life on the line daily to treat strangers. She was at work this morning, despite the fact that she spent the night in Acute Care Unit with her sick baby. I am not here to tell you how to run the pharmacy – I just want to know if you can help her."

"Hey! You don't need to shout." KK had not realized it, but everyone had gone quiet and was looking at them.

"There might be some set aside for Private Wing. I will check." The pharmacist motioned for them to wait in his office while he went into a back store. In a short while he came back. "Do you have a prescription?"

Kakayi pulled a medical form from her pocket. It was the prescription from Acute Care unit. The pharmacist glanced at it but did not touch it. He went to his desk, counted out the dose, and handed Kakayi the medicine. They thanked him and walked out. None of the other people in the pharmacy said anything as they exited. When they got to the corridor, Kakayi started to thank KK again. "Take the medicine to Acute Care and stay with the child till she is better," KK said, before running up the stairs two at a time to head back to the A&E.

***

Ntege heard about the strike from his mechanic. As he closed the bonnet of the old Toyota, he asked if Ntege was one of the doctors staying away from work that day. "No. Why?"

"They said on the news that the negotiations for better pay have failed, so the doctors have vowed not to return to work."

"Hmm...," grunted Ntege. "You know Mulago never closes. I am sure a few doctors will stay on and work." But as he drove through the hospital gate it occurred to him that if indeed the strike was on, he would have no junior doctors on duty. Not good. The last time that happened, he had had to do the work of the interns, and the kind of operations that he had not done since his PG room days. He was sympathetic to the Senior House Officers, and prayed that their pay would be increased, but he did not hold out much hope. The government had lied through every strike there had been about better pay and better working conditions. As far as Ntege could see, the only thing that ever changed was the faces of the officers lying on behalf of the government. A long line of ministers, permanent secretaries, and directors of medical services read from the same script. Government did not need to be creative because by the beginning of the next serious strike, it was always a new generation of interns, or house officers, so the lies always came across as sincere to them. He was still thinking about this when he entered the Accident & Emergency department. It was only 2.00pm yet the ward was already crowded. An intern was bending over a patient in the corner. At least he had one doctor to work with.

***

The side room of Ward 4B was designed as a lab. There must have been a time when specimens were examined here, but that time was surely long gone. The current occupants were graduate students specializing in internal medicine. This was now the PG room. The lock on the door did not work, the windows had layers of dirt that made the glass look glazed, and the chairs were bulky and too low for the high workbench. The students had found stools that served them better. Here they spent their spare time away from the ward, reading, looking at radiographs and lab results, and discussing whatever patients presented diagnostic or treatment challenges. One of their interesting patients was Hasule up in Psychiatry, Ward 16. Every medical student for the last one decade knew him, and he in turn knew many of the doctors. The most intriguing thing about him was how he made things up convincingly. Unsuspecting new students rotating in psychiatry often believed him before they were introduced to his diagnosis.

Hasule casually referred to his recent visit to State House to meet with the President, and his phone calls with the Inspector General of Police. None of this was true, but how was anyone to know, when he spun the tale to explain why he was now not allowed to leave the country, and why his passport was in the custody of the Internal Security Organisation. He had, he would continue, dropping his voice a notch to cut off the inevitable eavesdroppers, come across some very sensitive security information linking the American government to the vicious oil wars in South Sudan. The students often walked away wondering why this fascinating man was in a mental health ward. They would soon discover that he suffered from schizophrenia, and that the unreal world he had created for himself was all part of the delusion of grandeur, a common symptom of the disease. Next to Hasule was Kagunywa, the patient with a split personality.

"A major risk factor for these mental health conditions must be working in government. The people in Ministry of Finance regularly make up economic figures that only they believe. When everyone else feels the inflation, they tell us that the economy is growing with rates in double digits. Government has been eradicating poverty successfully for decades, yet clearly, the poor are getting poorer and more plentiful," Agaba, the latest resident to rotate in psychiatry said.

"The Finance guys are only spewing out what the President instructs them to. When it comes to making things up I think our Fountain of Honor is the worst offender," Namubiru added.

"Sounds to me more like the Fountain of Horror ..." mused Agaba.

"To his credit I do not think he really makes things up. Maybe those around him feel obliged to do so. I believe his problem is entirely different. Clearly, he suffers from a classic split personality. We do well to understand that at any one time, we are listening to one of the personalities, and the other personality might not know, or even agree with what he is saying. When he says something that contradicts an earlier position, he is not confused or dishonest. It is just a different personality now speaking." Dr. Namisi had a way of making his opinion sound like the final word on any subject.

"Guys! You do realize that this conversation is treasonous, right? Accusing the President of a mental health condition…" Okudi was very averse to making any negative comments on government generally, and on the President especially.

"Don't be ridiculous! Who does not know that the President talks out of both sides of his mouth? The mistake that most people make is to conclude that he is a liar. Maybe occasionally he does lie, but most of the time the seeming contradictions are positions of different personalities. So what is worse? To accuse him of dishonesty or to acknowledge that he has a mental health problem? A split personality is a psychiatric disorder, not a crime."

"I am out of here. When you end up behind bars I will not be coming to see you." Okudi picked up his clinical coat and left the room. Agaba, Namubiru, and Namisi were quiet for a short while. The class was sharply divided along political lines.

"Not to belabor the point, I do think that we are dealing with a narcissistic personality disorder." Agaba was not letting Namisi win on this one. "The sense of self-importance and superiority, manipulation and use of other people, need for admiration and praise … to believe that you, and only you out of millions of capable adults can solve the problems of a country."

"It could be a secondary diagnosis," Namisi responded, sounding only partially persuaded. "And he would be in good company. Many great leaders have suffered from these very conditions.[20] Emperor

---

[20] Matthew C Keller and Peter M Visscher. Genetic variation links creativity to psychiatric disorders. *Nat Neurosci*. 2015 July; 18(7): 928–929. doi:10.1038/nn.4047.

Nero, Joseph Stalin, Abraham Lincoln, Winston Churchill, Mobutu Sese Seko, ... they all suffered serious mental illnesses. Oh. And perhaps the most infamous of them all – it is believed that Adolf Hitler suffered from borderline personality disorder and narcissistic personality."

"The problem with that thinking though, is that people then excuse plain and simple greed for political power. Leaders need to be held accountable. Besides, Mobutu and great should not be in the same sentence." The room was again silent for a while.

"By the way, has anyone seen the new ads trying to woo tourists and foreign investors to Uganda? I saw one on CNN. Very well done, but they must cost a hefty sum – both the design and airing on such a channel." Namubiru was eager to change the subject.

"Namubiru, where do you get time to watch CNN?"

"It was run on NTV, but someone told me it was airing on CNN as well. Anyway, pretty cool. Pearl of Africa, gifted by nature and all that. It makes you feel proud to be Ugandan."

"I will throw up if I hear another person waxing lyric about Uganda while misquoting Winston Churchill's endorsement of the country as the Pearl of Africa. For one, it was another Englishman, Henry Stanley, who coined the expression in the late 1800s. Churchill, to who the phrase is wrongly attributed, came much later, and in his famous 1908 publication he merely repeated what Stanley had said."

It was always surprising how much history Namisi could spew out, and he did not tire of reminding his friends that he got a distinction in the subject in school. The information often sounded too precise for something remembered from high school history classes of a decade earlier, but it always checked out.

"Anyhow, whichever imperialist explorer described Uganda's natural beauty; it does not explain why the Queen did not move the seat of her Empire here, if the English were so impressed with it. The point was, and remains, that this lovely corner of God's creation is at best a source of raw materials, a reservoir of cheap and increasingly unwelcome labor, and a brief stop for the more adventurous Europeans to soak in the sun. That is, before the threat of malaria and other life threatening tropical diseases reminds them of the equally beautiful but far safer Scottish countryside. So – the government can pour all the money they want into fake ads made up of fake imperialist quotes, but unless they deal with the corruption, and show genuine commitment to growing the economy as opposed to lining the pockets of regime supporters, every investor will run off after only a brief visit. Those that choose to stay are thieves." Namisi picked up his clinical coat and said something about a teaching up in the Heart Institute before leaving the room. Agaba left shortly after.

Namubiru, now left alone, wished that her colleagues would not take politics so seriously. Post-graduate studies were hard enough; one did not need to spice them up with political friction with one's colleagues. Discussions in Medicine were far more enjoyable, but lately any discussion had a way of turning political. She had been a regular contributor to the hot discussions, which were initially all in good humour, but lately something had shifted. Okudi was avoiding the PG room, and Namisi was not much fun anymore. Agaba's seat on the fence was rocking back and forth; he would soon have to decide which way to jump. They all took things too seriously. Namubiru tried to lighten things up as much as possible.

***

From its beginning in 1924 until 1989, Makerere remained the only medical school in Uganda. If one met a Ugandan doctor that had trained in the country, they could safely assume that he or she was a product of Makerere Medical School. In 1989 however, Mbarara University of Science and Technology opened its doors to their pioneering class of medical students, breaking Makerere's monopoly on medical education. This additional capacity increased the numbers of doctors graduating, but both institutions struggled with extreme under-funding. Makerere had been functioning in this sub-optimal state for so long that there were now members of faculty who had never known adequate resource levels. Equipment that was taken for granted elsewhere was only seen in books here. Besides, there were growing pressures for the school to increase its intake. Prof. Nelson Sewankambo, a product of Makerere's undergraduate and master of medicine programs, was now at the helm of the institution, and this was to become his battle.

Sewankambo was famous for his insistence that student numbers remain low for as long as the training facilities were not expanded. He argued that the 120 students being admitted into the medical program every year were the most the school could take and still ensure a well-trained medical graduate. "The day we increase our intake with the current level of resources is the day the quality of our products will begin to go down." It was not just the physical space, he often pointed out, but the teaching staff, labs and reagents, operating rooms and student supplies, and the opportunities for students to interact with and have hands-on training with the patients. One year his conviction was to be tested in dramatic fashion.

The Advanced Level results were out, and the medical school's cut-off points were well known. The top one hundred and twenty students were selected. As a matter of procedure though, the proposed list for admission was usually presented to the University Admissions Board, which had the final say. At this Board, Sewankambo presented his list and showed the top 120 students who were being considered for admission to the medical school. He was surprised when one of the other Board members suggested that he consider admitting a few more students. "No. Those are the numbers we can manage with our current level of resources," Sewankambo responded.

"But surely, you can take a few more? Say six more students," the colleague pressed.

"Look. We have discussed the issue of increasing the intake extensively both here and in the School Board, and we are not persuaded that we can do it just yet."

"So maybe you can take just one more student."

Suddenly it occurred to Sewankambo that this was not the usual random pressure for the school to swell its numbers. There was a very specific interest here. He remained quiet.

Another colleague spoke up. "Nelson, student number 126 on the list is my son. Please help me."

The room went quiet. All eyes were on Sewankambo. He felt trapped. Clearly, he was the only one who had been unaware of the matter. Nobody spoke. People started fidgeting with their stacks of papers. They were shifting in their chairs. "Gentlemen, I cannot do what you are asking. This is not about me. It is about what is fair. I cannot possibly take the sixth student down the list and reject the five ahead of him. And I cannot take all six, we do not have the space and resources for them. If I did that, it would get all of us in trouble. So for all our sakes, I kindly request that we leave the admission list as it is."

Still, nobody spoke. Now people were looking down, not wanting to look at either Sewankambo, or the father whose son was going to look for another university, or another career.

Sewankambo spoke again. "I am sorry. I think it is best that we keep this straight. If it was my son, I would expect you to do the same."

The Deputy Vice Chancellor came to everyone's rescue. "Well! Medicine is closed, let us move on to the next faculty." The tension broke. And with it probably a relationship. That was the extent of Sewankambo's almost fanatical determination to keep students' numbers matched with the available resources for teaching and learning. But days were coming when all this fine logic would be abandoned, and they were not too far in the future.

***

In 2004, Makerere seemed to have found the perfect solution to the decades-old teaching and learning problems in Medicine: Problem-Based Learning (PBL). It was proposed by Prof. Sam Luboga who worked as Deputy Dean in charge of Education, and was supported by a training grant through 'innovation @ Makerere'. Luboga had tried to introduce it unsuccessfully ten years before after seeing how well it worked at MacMaster University in Canada. This time round however, his success was unprecedented. It was so instantly welcomed, and generated such enthusiasm that his initial proposal to pilot it in just the one program (Bachelor of Medicine & Surgery) was rejected. Five programs, including Dentistry, embraced it all at ago. He was later to quip that it was the euphoria of novelty that drove the process. Five champions were chosen: Prof. Sam Luboga, Dr. Sarah Kiguli, Dr. Stephen Kijjambu, Dr. Moses Galukande, Dr. Andrew Mwanika. These leaders went to Maastricht, Netherlands, and got trained in order to drive the full and effective transition from the old style of teaching and learning – with its reliance on lectures as the main means of knowledge transfer – to the new problem-based learning.

Makerere could not have picked more persuaded, or more committed pioneers. On its return, the team indeed oversaw the adoption of the approach, with its related Community Based Education and Service (COBES) component. The first two years were a roaring success. Commenting on the transformational power of the new educational approach, the team was told that Makerere University had been good, it was now about to become great. The optimism was palpable. But when the novelty wore off, especially after it became evident that the change would not put any more money in the pockets of the faculty that were taking on this very intensive approach, the excitement rapidly cooled off. Many people grumbled, and some quietly withdrew their participation, leaving students on their own. A few people were outright hostile. Eye specialist and prolific writer Medi Kawuma, who had been among the early proponents, now turned sharp critic. He churned out vitriolic letter upon vitriolic letter to anyone who would listen, including the Speaker of Parliament, the Inspector General of Government, the head of Police, and the President! The letters called for help to put an end to the disaster that had befallen medical education at Makerere. Students were not learning, the critics claimed, because lecturers had been stopped from teaching, and had been turned into mere tutors. The opposition to PBL was harsh and unrelenting.

***

Except for northern Uganda where the twenty years of armed conflict have no equal, it is a matter for debate whether anything has disrupted development, decimated communities, and changed the destinies of entire populations as much as AIDs has, since the end of slave trade – and for Uganda there are a number of contenders for this notoriety, such as the eight years of Idi Amin. But catastrophic as the pandemic has been, AIDS created a whole new economy that grew and thrived, even as people continued to die. First, there were the clinicians who quickly realized that they were onto something big – something far beyond themselves, beyond Uganda. Something at once frightening and monstrous, something impossible to contain, that begged to be respected and understood. Very quickly followed the public health people. Historically, public health was the poor relative at Makerere Medical School. Most people did not consider it medicine at all. It was understood that if one wanted to remain in medicine and in academia, they did not apply to join the Institute of Public Health. That was for those content to spend their days teaching communities about good nutrition and the value of a latrine. That, it was agreed, did not require too much academic rigor. The public health diploma took all of nine months to complete, compared to the three years for a master's degree in medicine.

Then comes AIDS. With the epidemic came new research and research grants. It did not take long for clinicians to figure out that while in the short run the research might not help their patients – there were no remedies for HIV and AIDS for more than a decade after its onset – the research grants did not hurt their financial fortunes. As the saying goes, those that set out to do good, did well. Some did so well that the AIDS work expanded to fill their entire workspace, and their lifetime careers. And as might be expected, this sudden and almost total focus on HIV and AIDS was at the expense of other areas of medicine. Soon, the top brains in any graduating class were heading, not to surgery or pediatrics, not even to internal medicine, but to epidemiology, and to – yes, public health. The AIDS economy was roaring, it was global, and Uganda had the unenviable reputation of being close to, if not at, the very heart of the epidemic. Where the 1970s saw the exodus of academics and health professionals following Idi Amin's infamous expulsion of Asians, the 1980s and 1990s saw, first a trickle, and then a steady stream of international researchers, before the dam burst to let in the flood in the early 2000s. Where in many European and American hospitals one might see one or two gay men with immunosuppression in several months, in Uganda there was an entire population begging to be studied. The President was being open about the HIV threat, and he was saying some right things most of the time.[21] The country had a fairly well-trained but barely-paid health workforce, eager to drop whatever they were doing to join paid research teams. Uganda was set to become the HIV and AIDS research capital of the world. It was a match made in global research heaven.

The noble, the ignoble, and the outright sinister were all headed for Uganda, and for every international agent that came, there were probably several Ugandans waiting to collaborate in the work. Rules were being made up as the work went along. There were ethical dilemmas at every turn – should doctors tell their patients that their spouses had the virus? Should doctors disclose their own HIV status to their patients? What did 'informed consent' mean when dying people were lining up to take whatever was being offered as a possible remedy? What did you do when a patient's choices were either a blood transfusion or death – and the blood probably had the virus in it? How were research grants to be managed? One professor hired his wife, a nurse, as the study coordinator. She supervised doctors, made payments, signed off and dispatched blood samples to foreign institutions, and only she and her husband knew what was in the

---

[21] President Museveni did not start off being open about HIV. Very early in the epidemic when Dr. Wilson Carswell, a British surgeon working at Mulago, wrote a research paper on 'Slim disease' based on his research in Rakai, he was asked to leave.

research grant budget. A few people frowned on this kind of unethical behavior, but that would soon be seen as kindergarten homework once the serious profiteering set in. It did not take long for Makerere to start topping the charts in the volume of research publications, never mind that at least initially; most of the lead authors were not Ugandans.

With time though, research started to pay off, both in terms of preventing infection, and treating established infections. After many false starts and the use of highly toxic and ineffective medicines, researchers gave the world the medicines that transformed HIV from a death sentence to a chronic disease. Anti-retroviral drugs, or ARVs as they became widely known, were literally life giving, to individuals, communities, and to countries like Uganda. Scientists in labs and hospitals around the world had worked for years against great odds to arrive at this success. Because the cost would have put the medicines out of reach of the millions of people that needed them, phenomenal efforts were made at global levels to avail the drugs either free or at greatly subsidized prices, and to put in place elaborate systems to get them safely to those in need. The stage was set for the dark side of the Ugandan AIDS economy to be brought to the fore.

As the clinical and public health researchers described the horrifying extent of the AIDS epidemic in the country – in some communities as many as one in every five people were said to be infected - and the extreme vulnerability of communities; as agencies like the World Health Organization and Global Fund (for HIV, Tuberculosis and Malaria) put together substantial sums of money to counter the disaster, highly placed individuals in the Ministry of Health readied themselves for the kill.

The looting of the Global Fund money in Uganda was not an impulsive grab of a few million shillings, or the systematic siphoning off of the infamous 'ten percent' by the financial managers of the grant, leaving the rest of the money to do the work. Even years after the scale of the theft was discovered, it still boggled the mind that it happened in the manner that it did, and that some of the perpetrators were walking about as free men and women, never having spent a day in jail.

In August 2005 the Global Fund announced that it was suspending all grant funding to Uganda, totaling US $367 million.[22] An audit by PriceWaterhouseCoopers had raised concerns of 'inappropriate expenditures and improper accounting' with regards to the Global Fund money. President Museveni set up a commission of inquiry in the mismanagement of the Fund. The public hearings held from September 2005 to April 2006 heard testimonies from more than 130 witnesses and reviewed some 500 exhibits tendered as evidence.[23] The public was appalled by what had happened. Key project managers had been irregularly appointed. The Minister of Health Jim Muhwezi was said to have negotiated with DFCU bank to exchange dollars at a lower-than-market rate so that they could pocket the difference. Junior minister of health Captain Mike Mukula, together with his two colleagues, were accused of siphoning hundreds of millions of Global Fund money for political mobilisation. Fictitious non-governmental organisations and companies had been set up as service providers, and payments were being shared without any work done. Even where some work happened, expenses were inflated and false receipts presented. Allowances going into tens of thousands of dollars had been paid out to ministers for supervision work that was not done. Justice James Ogoola who headed the Commission called the Fund's management "a pile of filth".[24,25]

The appointment of the Commission of Inquiry might not have recovered much money, but it had the desired effect on the donors. Richard Feachem, then executive director of the Global Fund, probably spoke too soon. "The openness and thoroughness with which President Yoweri Museveni

---

[22] The Global Fund Welcomes Ugandan Corruption Inquiry Report. https://www.theglobalfund.org/en/news/2006-06-02-the-global-fund-welcomes-ugandan-corruption-inquiry-report/

[23] The New Humanitarian. Uganda: Misuse of funds revealed as global fund inquiry quizzes ministers. 24 Mar 2006

[24] IRIN / PlusNews. Uganda: Global Fund probe reveals massive graft. 03 April 2006. https://reliefweb.int/report/uganda/uganda-global-fund-probe-reveals-massive-graft accessed 09 July 2019

[25] David Wendt. $12 Million Lost, But Has Anything Changed for the Global Fund in Uganda? Center for Global Development. 14 November, 2008. (https://www.cgdev.org/blog/12-million-lost-has-anything-changed-global-fund-uganda accessed 9 July 2019)

addressed the Global Fund's concerns about the management of the grants it finances in Uganda has set an example for how allegations of corruption should be dealt with. By conducting a public inquiry under the competent leadership of Justice Ogoola, Uganda has given a clear message that abuse of money meant for those suffering the consequences of malaria and AIDS is unacceptable," wrote Feachem, Executive Director of the Global Fund, 2006.[26]

The health sector was still reeling from the Global Fund scandal when it came to light that the same leadership at the Ministry of Health had superintended over another colossal loss, this time with money from GAVI (Global Alliance for Vaccines and Immunization) meant for the country's immunization program.

***

On Thursday 26 April 2007, Brigadier Noble Mayombo was ill enough to accept an admission to Kololo Hospital, a private hospital in the heart of Kololo. The doctors diagnosed acute pancreatitis, a raging inflammation of the pancreas, a small organ in the depths of the abdomen that makes digestive juices. The following day his condition continued to worsen, prompting his doctors to transfer him to International Hospital Kampala, where he was immediately admitted to the Intensive Care Unit. Here, despite the most sophisticated medical interventions that the ICU could offer, it was evident that Mayombo's pancreas was disintegrating and destroying other organs in the process. By Sunday 29 April 2007 he had slipped into coma and was on life-support. The doctors were under tremendous pressure to do any and everything necessary to fix Mayombo's health. He was only 42 years old, was among the most powerful men in the country, and had, as far as the public was concerned, enjoyed perfect health until the current sudden illness. He held the very sensitive position of Permanent Secretary for the Ministry of Defense, was the Board Chair of the New Vision Corporation, and was known to be a close confidant of the President. He had previously headed the dreaded Chieftaincy of

---

[26] Peter Nyanzi. Uganda: Global Fund Praises Museveni Over Probe. *The Monitor* 2 June 2006.

Military Intelligence (CMI). There had been talk in some circles of his being a possible successor to President Museveni.

As though to remind the doctors that this was no ordinary patient, there was security presence everywhere in the hospital, including the ICU itself. There were uniformed officers in the parking lot, there were uniformed and plain-clothes security agents in the corridors, and close family and trusted colleagues camped at the entrance of the ICU. In the quiet room with patient monitors beeping constantly, Mayombo lay motionless, unaware of the drama unfolding around him. And if there was drama in the hospital, there was even more drama outside the hospital, with conspiracy theories flying around Kampala and beyond. 'Mayombo has been poisoned! The doctors are trying to figure out how to neutralize the poison,' went one of the stories. It was said that the doctors working on Mayombo were under surveillance.

The doctors held frequent meetings in the ICU to review his status, and to determine if anything should be changed or added. A doctor from State House checked in constantly to get updates of Mayombo's progress. Plans were already underway to fly him to Israel. A team at a top hospital in Israel had been contacted, and they were waiting to receive him. Because his condition was deteriorating very rapidly however, Israel started to look unlikely. Nairobi was a more realistic destination. Mayombo was on a respirator, his systems were being closely monitored, and he was on medications to keep his major organs from shutting down. Nairobi was at least 45 minutes away by the presidential Gulfstream, but on either end of the flight were the most hazardous segments of the journey. He would have to be moved into the most advanced ambulance available, and the journey from IHK in Namuwongo to Entebbe would be rough. The first five hundred meters from IHK in any direction alone would be a test to less critical patients. Kampala roads, even when paved, were notoriously narrow and irregular. An ambulance ride for the acutely inflamed abdomen and an evolving multiple organ failure was going to be a very high risk transfer, but IHK had considerable experience evacuating critically ill patients. Once the decision was made, the wheels were set in motion. Aga Khan Hospital in Nairobi was contacted, detailed consultations were done, and evacuation plans shifted to Nairobi, at least initially. Having done all that they could, the IHK doctors prayed that their patient would make it to their Kenyan colleagues no worse than when he left them.

***

Kweete half sat and half lay on the bench outside the Heart Institute. She was surrounded by other patients and their relatives, all impatiently waiting for the clinic to open. The Institute was located on the ground floor of the hospital. It was nestled between the main operating rooms on one side, and the mortuary on the other. One giving hope, the other taking it away. Kweete had been to the institute enough times to know the routine. The nurses opened the door and collected the appointment cards from the waiting patients. Their files were retrieved, and they were then called in one by one, often depending on their order of arrival. As they waited, the less critically ill patients often struck up conversation. Today the topic of interest was the hospital renovations. A gentleman that sounded very knowledgeable told the rest that because the Queen of England was coming to attend a meeting in Kampala, Mulago Hospital was going to get a complete face lift. A lot of new equipment was being installed.

"New equipment will be wonderful, but unless the charges are reduced nobody will use it. We are already paying too much money for the old equipment. Will the charges not be higher?" an older lady rejoined.

"We hear some people do not pay. They come here with chits from State House and they are treated free."

The knowledgeable man was called in and the conversation changed to the cost and quality of food at the many eateries surrounding the hospital.

"Kweetegyeka?" a nurse called from the doorway. Kweete got up, gathered her belongings, and followed the nurse. She was relieved to see the same doctor that had seen her the previous two visits.

"How are you doing?" he asked, signaling for her to get onto the examination couch.

She had been rather tired lately. He ordered for a new type of test called an Echo scan. She would have to go and get it done at a private hospital in town; Mulago's machine was not working. By the time she got back the clinic would be closed, so she would have to return the following week for the doctor to look at the test results. She hoped that after the Queen's visit the hustle of looking for functional equipment in private hospitals would be over.

***

On Tuesday 1 May 2007, Noble Mayombo died at the Aga Khan Hospital in Nairobi, due to complications of acute pancreatitis. There were still rumors swirling around that he might have been poisoned. They were fueled by the brevity of his illness and the uncommon nature of the diagnosis – many people had never heard of pancreatitis, and there was no equivalent in local languages. Mayombo had lived by the sword, so to say, and many were willing to believe that he had died by the sword. He had made enough enemies in his time as CMI chief, and his closeness to the President and the possibility that he might be gunning for the big office ahead of more senior aspirants meant that some people were not entirely unhappy about his early demise. They said Noble Mayombo was the unrepentant author of many ignoble acts. Ironically, some of the accusing fingers pointed to the President himself, who was said to be intolerant of political ambition, and wary of Mayombo's wit and popularity.

***

The news of Mayombo's death was discussed at length in the surgeons' boardroom. The consensus was that the referral was medically unwarranted, but politically inevitable. Had Mayombo died in a Ugandan hospital, there would have been a sense that he might have survived had he been at a better hospital. Yet no politician was coming right out to say that Ugandan hospitals were ill equipped, and that at least in Mayombo's case, a better equipped facility would have been preferable to a trip on the Gulfstream.

"In Uganda every important person who dies suddenly has been the victim of foul play. Nobody wants to believe that they have died an ordinary death. Mayombo was abusing alcohol for years. Why should an acute pancreatitis be a surprise?"

"It's the odds. There are many people Mayombo's age hitting the bottle regularly. Why should he be the one to die?"

"I think the question should be why not. If there is an afterlife, he is now busy reuniting with those he sent on ahead of himself while he worked as CMI Chief. Many people met their untimely deaths at his behest." Clearly, there were not too many tears being shed here.

"I was waiting to see how many caskets there would be at his funeral service," Ntege said.

"Why? Were there more deaths?"

"No, but that would complete the folly. It seems an anticlimax for someone that routinely moved in a motorcade to be buried in one coffin with no escorts." And with that Ntege turned back to whatever he was reading in his corner. It was always hard to know whether he said certain things in jest or in earnest.

The conversation turned to the quality of health care in general. Baka, addressing himself to nobody in particular, asked, "So – how are we doing now that the ministry is safely back in the hands of doctors?"

"Safely, did you say?" Francis, who had not seemed the least bit interested in the conversation jumped in. "Have our fortunes been dependent on the profession of the man or woman at the wheel? The deterioration was clearly established before the lawyer and pilot took the reins. Or should I say before the pilot entered the cockpit? Except for the fact that the biggest robbery of health sector funds up until that point happened under their watch, I do not think they were any worse than their medically qualified predecessors."

"Really? Are you saying you see nothing amiss in an airplane pilot being the chief supervisor of health services? Granted, the minister need not have a master's degree in health services management, but maybe a brush with the profession would help. I don't think that Mukula or Muwhezi knew which end of the syringe held the needle. Much less why it was critical to have a working refrigerator in a health center. I can imagine the conversation with the staff in their first week at the ministry." Francis put on a high-pitched feminine voice. "Mr. Minister sir, we are having problems maintaining the vaccine cold chain. We need more money allocated to it; otherwise we risk another measles epidemic."

Francis dropped the high-pitched voice for a deep male voice with a Western Uganda accent. "Cold chain? I thought you used vaccines to prevent measles. I can imagine that chains might come in handy in psychiatry, but should health workers not be able to restrain the kids for immunization without resorting to chains?"

The high-pitched voice again. "Sir, it is not a physical chain. A cold chain is a technical term ... a kind of ... well; it is ... a manner of speech."

"You need money to pay for a manner of speech? A theory? No wonder - I have been told that there is a lot of wastage in this ministry!"

"Francis!" Baka interrupted the monologue. "These were highly educated men. They might not be doctors, but they were not dumb."

"Yes. And a whole lot of good their brilliance has done us." Just then, Winnie opened the door and announced in her usual dramatic fashion, "Guys! Do you know the entire university is on strike? What are you doing here? You are the traitors!" If she had not become a doctor, Winnie could have had a career in acting. She had a way of converting the ordinary into the spectacular.

"So what are *you* doing here?"

"Getting my stuff and heading home. Those of you paid by the Ministry of Health can carry on working. Those of us under Makerere are on strike until further notice."

***

In reality, the now-on, now-off university strikes made little difference to the surgeons, and had no effect on the occupants of PG rooms. These doctors could be relied upon to work around the year, no matter what was happening elsewhere. But the latest spate of strikes had finally pointed a finger at the medics, accusing them of weakening the otherwise unified front by university workers in their quest for more decent pay.

"What I don't get though, is why the rest of Ugandans do not rise up to join us when we strike. Surely, it should be obvious to them that the strikes are primarily about patients. That we are trying to compel the government to provide better health care. But quite often what one hears is criticism about doctors abandoning patients to die."

"True. It is a case of the kidneys telling the failing heart that it is the heart's problem. Soon enough the kidneys will know why the heart was begging for help. By that time, the kidneys will be closing shop. Most Ugandans have failed to connect the dots between doctors' welfare and their own welfare."

"To be fair, I think people do realise that it is not hospitals and doctors that keep populations healthy. It is farmers and teachers; it is city planners, and water and sewerage engineers. We overestimate our own importance."

"Right! Please tell me which farmer to refer you to for your prostate problems. How many of your arthritis patients have you referred to a city planner? The Ministry of Health is being dishonest when they say that they are focusing on preventive medicine as an explanation for the neglect of doctors and hospitals. In fact, they are doing neither prevention nor care. A lot of talk, no action. It has become the Ministry of Hype and Sick."

***

The weekly departmental meeting was dominated by the preparations for the Commonwealth Heads of Government Meeting, scheduled to take place in Kampala in November 2007. Mulago Hospital would be the main hub in a network of hospitals to be on high alert, should any of the guests or service people need medical attention during the course of the summit. A large number of local and international journalists were expected to descend on the city, and Uganda was going to be in the glare of the cameras. The hospital administration had asked the various departments to make lists of the items that they needed in order to be adequately prepared. They had all been waiting for a chance such as this. Dr. Edward Ddumba, the Executive Director of the hospital, was chair of the committee on emergency medical services for the entire summit. What the government had been unwilling or unable to avail to Ugandans, they were now falling over themselves to procure for the foreign guests. The most important guest was going to be Queen Elizabeth, the Head of the Commonwealth.

> Francis had been quiet through the discussions. Now that the formal meeting was over, the real debate was beginning. He started seriously enough. "The Queen of England is coming to town, and you would think that it was a groom coming to get his bride. Uganda is preening her feathers in anticipation. The President has given the nod to the Ministry of Finance to pay for all manner of ridiculous irrelevances. But this is no ordinary love affair. The Queen is the reigning English monarch and head of the most dominant slave trader of the eighteenth and nineteenth centuries, coming to visit

the relatives and descendants of slaves.[27] Does that not make for an interesting conversation?"

Before anyone would answer, Francis broke out into a chuckle. "Picture the President, leaning forward, clearing his voice and wearing his signature smile." Francis dropped his voice and put on an exaggerated Western Uganda accent.

"Yes Your Majesty. Our country is suffering from severe human resource shortages because of all those people who were sold as slaves by your subjects. But we have upgraded our hospitals for your visit, in case any of your people get a medical emergency. The head of these services is British trained."

Then he paused and raised his voice a notch to imitate a female with a nasal English accent.

"No thank you, Your Excellency, that will not be necessary. I understand that neither you, nor your immediate and extended families use the local hospitals. We have taken the precaution to

---

[27] It is estimated that between 1450 and the early 19th century, up to 28 million Africans were forcibly sold into slavery, and mostly sent to the Americas. Britain was the dominant slave trader, transporting more than 300,000 Africans a year in chains on overcrowded and disease-ridden boats. As many as one in 10 died from illness, suicide or starvation. A protracted campaign finally persuaded the British Parliament to pass an act abolishing slavery in 1807. It was abolished throughout the British Empire in 1833. Among those campaigning for the abolition of slave trade were African former slaves Oladuah Equiano (c.1745-c.1797) and Ignatius Sancho (1729-1780). Their contributions have gone largely unacknowledged, although they were active in the same time period as the better known William Wilberforce (1759-1833), who for 18 years annually tabled anti-slavery motions in Parliament. Wilberforce died in July 1833. In August 1833 the slave trade was abolished. It is not known how many people were taken out of the territory that became present day Uganda. The year 2007 when Uganda hosted the Commonwealth Heads of Government Meeting (CHOGM) marked the bicentenary (200th) anniversary of the abolition of slave trade. It was an opportunity for the global community to call upon Britain to formally apologize for the role of the British Empire in slave trade, and to propose tangible reparations. In Uganda the subject of reparations was not on the agenda. The only lasting memory of that 200th anniversary is that of the massive corruption that characterized the procurement of the services related to the meeting.

The Patient

bring our own medical team." He opened his eyes wide and tilted his head towards the invisible queen. In a stage whisper, with a knowing smile on his face, he said, "It's true Your Majesty, even I do not trust some of our people. Many of them are still sleeping. As you know all my grandchildren have been delivered in London. It is safer there." The 'sleeping' came out as '*sleep-inj*'.

High pitched English accent again. "Is it true, Your Excellency, that the hospital which my cousin opened at Uganda's independence 45 years ago is still the largest in the country? If my memory serves, the population then was less than 8 million. Now I am informed that it is closer to 40 million." A gentle frown formed across Francis' royal brow. "It does get a trifle crowded in there, does it not?"

The President, now turning defensive, responded. "Yes, it is the largest, but we have expanded the services. We expanded the mortuary, and we gave the hospital a new fence. A very big task that was; the fence." Francis spread his arms and opened his eyes wide for emphasis. He would have carried on with the monologue, but Kitya interjected.

"On a serious note, can anyone explain why we are trying to put on a pretense about the state of our health services? Does anyone imagine that there is even the remotest chance that any important person could show up here in Mulago for treatment? No!"

"Oh. So you do not want us to use the opportunity to improve our services? There are some items that we must get now, or we can forget about ever getting them. If we do not get the autoclaves for instance, I cannot imagine that there will be another opportunity in the near future. So forget the Queen and the foreign journalists. We must get these things for ourselves."

The room was quiet for a long while. Francis resumed. "Funny. Our ancestors were forcibly put in chains, loaded on ships and ferried to Europe and America. Today, centuries after the slave trade was officially abolished, we sell family land, abandon our families, and line up for days in search of visas to Europe and America. Visas top the prayer lists for miracles in many churches. I tell you what. If the US embassy said that anyone willing to wear chains between here and America would be given permanent residence once on the other side, there would be a stampede to get into the chains."

"Francis! What kind of mind comes up with such thoughts?"

"Oh. Now it is my mind? What about the minds of those who have robbed the country blind, and gotten it to the point at which educated young people dream of going to foreign countries to work as retirement home help? What minds do those people have?"

Kaggwa gathered his books, picked up his coat and quietly left the room. It had been hardly a month since his sister left for the USA on a visitor's visa, but she had just informed him in jubilation that she had already been 'fixed' at a job in an old people's home. She had a nursing degree, but her main job since graduation two years previously had been selling food supplements from office to office. Even working seven days a week she had not made enough money to afford her own place. A few short stints at private clinics had left her disillusioned by her daily encounters with desperation, malpractice, improvisation, and lack. Kaggwa knew that for young people like his sister, migrating to the USA was more dignified than staying at home. Kaggwa's quiet exit was not lost on Francis and Kitya.

"You really are insufferable!" Kitya resumed the discussion. "Of course neither the Queen nor the President has any illusions that the relationship between the two countries is one based on a common heritage. Today Uganda is a member of the Commonwealth, which is itself a curious name since there is no common wealth between the 53 countries under the flimsy umbrella that covers Britain's former colonies. Britain is said to be one of Uganda's closest development partners – another strange term, probably coined to avoid the more misleading terms of 'donor' and 'aid recipient', when for a long time Uganda has been donating to Britain. A little guilt here, a little greed

The Patient

there, a respectable theatre of contracts and Foreign Service jobs. A trade imbalance as old as the relationship."

***

The Monday morning departmental meeting was over and many of the surgeons were already gone. Only a handful lingered on, perhaps giving the out-patient clinics and operating rooms time to set up for the day.

"The World Health Organization has discovered a new disease," Kitya announced.

"In Uganda?" Karungi sounded doubtful.

"No. It is global. But Uganda is one of the worst affected countries. In fact we are the enviable hosts of the first ever global summit on this condition.[28, 29] It is called the 'health workforce brain drain'. I am not sure if we should be excited to host the summit, or sad that we qualify to host it."

"Hmm... I always wonder how venues for such meetings are determined. In this case though, I think the organisers chose well. Uganda knows a lot about brain drain – she is not just one of the worst affected countries, she has learnt how to actively promote the vice. Faced with a leaking roof, Uganda will quickly locate the source of the leak, widen it, and create a few other holes in its vicinity. In fact, I suspect that during the summit our ministers will be busy cutting deals with their wealthier counterparts on how to ship our health workers over." Karungi and Kitya were spurring on familiar ground.

"Guys, venues are not determined based on the prevalence of the problem," Baka interjected. Most global meetings on poverty, food insecurity, pharmaceutical shortages, and even malaria are held in

---

[28] Uganda hosts brain drain summit http://news.bbc.co.uk/2/hi/in_depth/7274661.stm accessed 9 September 2017
[29] New Vision. Brain drain in Africa is inevitable. 6 March 2008.

the wealthy capitals of the world, far removed from the subjects under discussion. I gather a lot of lobbying is involved to draw an important meeting to a country. The meeting comes with jobs, money, travel, and networking opportunities. In Uganda's case it might even precipitate further brain drain. The success of the meeting is not judged by whether or not it solves the problem. It is the numbers of participants, the involvement of so-called high-level speakers and dignitaries, the quality of the accommodation and champagne, and the images and gloss on the final report. Besides – does the Bible not say that to those who have, more will be given? And that those who have not, even the little they have will be taken away? The brain drain dilemma is totally biblical." Baka had a Bible verse for every situation.

"There you go! That is why they say we are driven by emotion rather than reason. Have you heard that some countries export skilled workers the same way we export coffee? We deliberately grow more than we need in order to sell it to countries that need it. So what is wrong with sending our excess health workers out there and getting foreign currency in return? What good is an excess of health workers here? Even if the money were to go directly to the workers' families, that is still revenue coming into the country."

"Except no Ugandan has died from a lack of coffee. When that begins to happen we shall advocate for a ban on coffee exports."

***

On 11 July 2010 football enthusiasts around the world were glued to their TV sets. It had been a month of adrenaline, late nights, bets won and lost, great excitement and the depths of disappointment, all in the roller coaster called the World Cup. For the first time in the history of the tournament, the African continent was playing host, and although the matches were being played in South Africa, the rest of the continent was acting as if it was in everyone's backyard. This was the African World Cup and 11 July was the *grand finale*.

On the World Cup Final night Robert Wangoda, a surgeon and acting Head of the Accident & Emergency Department at Mulago Hospital, was not watching the game. He was slouched in front of the TV at home, unwinding from his long day at the hospital, and thinking for the nth time that he ought to get up and make his way to bed. Then the newsreader on *Al-Jazeera* said something that jolted him into full alert. He sat up straight and tried to figure out if this was fresh news, or if the program was recounting something from the past. The words were clear enough but their significance took a while to sink in. A bomb blast had just occurred at Kyadondo Rugby Club in Kampala, where, from the news report, a huge crowd of football fans had gathered to watch the World Cup final. From the newsroom, the camera went to an anchor in Kampala, who confirmed that at least two blasts had happened, one at an Ethiopian restaurant in Kabalagala, and shortly after, a much larger one at the rugby sportsground. It was too soon to know how many people were injured, but the armed forces were already securing the two venues and taking the injured to Mulago Hospital.

Wangoda's heart was racing. He could not begin to imagine what the Accident & Emergency Department was going to be like once the Police trucks and Red Cross ambulances started arriving at the hospital. At the best of times, it was always a stretch when they received many injured people all at once. There were very few health workers on night duty: one doctor, a couple of nurses, maybe three people in the emergency theatre. All others were available on an on-call basis. He was all the way in Budo, some 15 kilometers away from the hospital. He dismissed the thought of driving to the hospital in the night almost as soon as it occurred to him. It would be unwise to go out on his own in a night like this. He would have to wait until morning to make his way there safely.

***

Dr. Moses Galukande, a surgeon working at Mulago and International Hospital Kampala (IHK), was watching the World Cup final at Humura Hotel, a short distance away from Mulago Hospital, on the night of 11 July 2010. The doctor on duty at IHK called to let him know that they had received two patients with what looked like grenade injuries. "Can you describe the injuries please?" Galukande asked.

"Both men have typical blast injuries, mostly to the head and chest. I think you want to come right away."

Galukande instructed the doctor to prepare the patients for emergency surgery. By the time he got to the hospital there were 12 patients waiting. It was obvious they were dealing with a mass casualty incident. The patients talked of an explosion at the Ethiopian Restaurant in Kabalagala, less than a kilometer away. News soon came through that there had been an even bigger blast at the Lugogo sports ground. Galukande activated the major incident response, and then went to theater to start working on the most critical patients. He would not emerge from the operating theatre for the next 48 hours.

IHK had developed its capacity over the years to respond to mass casualties. They had done drills regularly since the days of the Commonwealth Heads of Government Summit three years before. Now that hard work paid off. As soon as the mass casualty incident was declared, other surgeons were called in. Dr. Ian Clark took over the coordinating role, and organized hospital ambulances to go and fetch patients from the bomb blast scenes. The main pharmacy, which was ordinarily closed at that hour, was opened to provide the necessary supplies. Wards were cleared of non-emergency cases. In a couple of hours all the operating rooms were busy, as was the X-ray department. Galukande periodically napped between cases, and he and the rest of the medical teams did not rest until all the patients had been stabilized. He did not dwell on the fact that had he chosen to watch the World Cup final at Lugogo, he could have been one of the patients.

***

On the night of the World Cup 2010 final, Jackie Mabweijano, an Accident & Emergency surgeon at Mulago, was on the phone with a former classmate who now worked at a hospital in Johannesburg. The friend told her he had been on standby the entire duration of the World Cup, and that the hospital had had several drills in the months and weeks leading to the tournament in readiness for any form of mass incident. But thankfully, he had added, nothing had happened. He said he was looking forward to the end of the season so that everyone could breathe easy. A short while after Jackie got off the phone, someone from Mulago called to say there had been a bomb blast at Lugogo, and that patients were being brought to her unit. "Could it be true?" Jackie wondered. Within minutes a second phone call came. Jackie grabbed her bag and coat and headed to Mulago, hoping she could sort it out in a few hours.

Jackie was the first senior doctor to arrive at the A&E, and she found the crowd beginning to gather. Efforts were already underway to get more staff to come in and help. She and the Sister-in-Charge went through 3B Emergency and cleared it of all patients that were not critical. She then came to the triage area and helped to sort patients for theater. The Red Cross and Police Patrol were still bringing more patients when she went to theater to start on the first cases. By that time, the hospital deputy director Isaac Ezati and anesthesiologist Cephas Mijumbi had arrived and they took over the coordination, opening main theatre so that more surgical teams could work. From thinking that she might be done in a few hours, Jackie was to be in the unit for 48 hours, during which time she operated, reviewed patients, napped between cases, and talked to patients and their relatives in a never-ending effort to make sense of the unfolding nightmare of death and destruction.

***

Wangoda hardly slept. In his mind's eye he could see the draft 'mass incident management plan' that he had discussed many times with one of his predecessors in the unit, Mr. Isaac Ezati. They had presented it to the Hospital Senior Management for endorsement, but it was never approved, much less implemented. Now the document lay at the bottom of a drawer in the office, and he wondered if anyone remembered its contents. There had been drills in collaboration with Civil Aviation Authority, but some of the key personnel who had participated in the drills had since left the unit.

By dawn, he was awake and dressed. The bomb blasts were the only news on all the radio stations. He made his way to the hospital, and before he reached the third floor on which the A&E was located, he could see that there was major drama. His fears were confirmed when he approached the entrance to the unit. For the first several minutes, he could not enter because of the crowds. It seemed like half of Kampala had come to the hospital. There were people everywhere –around the Police Post, in the parking, the ambulance bay, and crowding the entrance to the A&E. There were some Police officers trying to control the crowds, but they did not seem to be having much success. People were crying, shouting into their phones, shouting at the health workers, or huddled in small groups. The chaos was unbelievable. He found patients lying on the bare floor, and he spotted nurses and some interns trying to put up IV lines on patients in the corridor. Some people were bending over patients, probably to comfort them, but equally likely to see if they knew them. It was hard to know which of these people swarming the A&E were being helpful and which ones were in the way.

He stood in the middle of the triage area and called everyone to attention. Initially nobody paid him any attention, but after a while, there was some lull in the noise levels. "Everyone, listen! We know you are all anxious to see your relatives and friends treated. We are equally anxious to do our work, but the doctors and nurses are not able to work on anyone with you crowding here. If you insist to stay here, we shall have to sit and wait. If you want us to work we kindly request that you all go outside. If you do not work in the A&E please go and wait outside. As soon as we are able to provide more information we shall pass it on."

People started to file out.

Someone had gone to the Nurses' Hostel and asked the student nurses to come and help. They came. They were the main hands in all the areas – cleaning, putting up IV lines, preparing patients for procedures, talking to relatives and trying to help people find their relatives … but many of them were also very new to nursing. Patients were dying, and the bodies would quickly be moved aside to make room for other patients to be assessed and managed.

The bulk of the injuries were to the head, neck and chest, confirming reports that the bomb had detonated a short distance off the ground into a largely seated crowd. There were relatively fewer injuries in the lower parts of the body. The head surgeons were going to be very busy. For the moment though, most of what was needed was order, efficient and continuing prioritization of the patients' needs for resuscitation and surgery, and plenty of space in which to lay out, examine, and treat patients.

Perhaps the most enduring memory of the second night for Jackie was coming out of theater to run into a friend who was looking for her sister, who she was convinced had been at Lugogo Sports ground. The friend had looked through the ward and had not found the sister. She asked Jackie if it was possible to go and look in the morgue. "I think so," Jackie responded. The friend begged Jackie to accompany her there. "Look, I have my hands full. But go on, I am sure someone over there will be able to help." The friend would not leave Jackie alone, and her distress was hard to ignore. Jackie excused herself and ran down the stairs with the friend to go and show her where the morgue was, past Ward 1C. On reaching there, the place was busy despite the hour. Even years later, Jackie could remember what happened. "We went inside. It was awful. ... Just awful. Row upon row of bodies. Dismembered bodies ... her sister was there. She had lost a leg. We came away numb. I had no time to mourn with her. I had to get back to theater."

Towards morning, Jackie came out of theater and sat in her office, put her feet up on a chair and tried to get some rest. An hour later, around 6.30 am she got up and the team started rounds to see who could be moved, and to carry on working. That morning a plane arrived from South Africa to evacuate some Americans who had been injured in the bomb blast, to take them to Johannesburg. In the meantime, the usual work of the unit did not stop. Road traffic crashes were still happening out there, children were still being burnt, hernias were still strangulating and coming to Mulago for care. It was the most stretched that the doctors could remember being. Day 2 went by and the roller coaster of patient assessment, care and loss continued. There were now a number of surgical teams with the specialists taking care of their patients – head injuries, eye injuries, some extremity injuries – it was a lot to work through.

On the third night, Jackie and Wangoda were finally able to go home. "I got home and slept right away because I was so exhausted. It was more like blacking out," Jackie recalled. "I remember weeks later Dr. Margaret Mungherera came and tried to give us some psychosocial support – a debriefing of the days following the bomb blast. We had not sat down to process what had happened to our patients, and to us. We were all traumatized. Some of us had worked in A&E for years, but that experience was different. And what about those poor student nurses who were seeing all those dead bodies ... and nobody told them how to feel or what to do? Maybe some left the training in shock. The hospital should have set up a corner right away, to help medical workers to deal with their emotions. Mungherera told people it was okay to cry, to feel angry, and to talk about our emotions so that we could work through them. But this debriefing was happening weeks after the event. The Police had reported that over 70 people died from the bomb blasts. I do not know how many people I saw die over those two days."

***

The Department of Surgery Board room was quiet. Over time, the room had morphed into office space. As more surgeons completed their training and left the PG room for the next group, the pressure for office space in the department became more intense. Initially surgeons shared offices, but that too became impractical beyond three surgeons per office. Some started to use the Board Room for the short periods between theater and clinics, or while waiting to teach a class. Eventually the Board Room turned into an open concept office that many young surgeons found convenient. It was here that the former occupants of PG room now took refuge. In the absence of a board, someone had put up a flipchart stand. But the magic of PG room was missing. The flipchart was used only infrequently, and mostly to illustrate a point during formal meetings.

***

Entebbe Municipality in Wakiso district had for decades boasted two hospitals only a few hundred feet apart: Entebbe Hospital Grade A and Entebbe Hospital Grade B. The names were left over from the colonial past, when whites did not share hospital space with blacks. The finer services available at grade A were inaccessible to the blacks whose facility was appropriately named grade B. Very subtle. But that was several decades ago, and any rational planning would have seen the two modest sized facilities merged and expanded to serve the ballooning population. For some reason they had been kept separate.

There had been talk in the press about the attempted take-over of the hospital but it had not been conclusive. It was often unclear whether the hospital was being taken over by State House, or the UPDF. The ambiguity was characteristic of the wide grey zone that involved the President's Office, the official residence of the Head of State, and the military. The three institutions seemed to have over time merged to the point where it was hard to tell one from the other. Resources meant for one often ended up in the other, and each of them had so-called classified expenditures whose main purpose was to probably avoid scrutiny, and to confound audits.

> Francis had been gone for most of the day. The top sheet on the corner flipchart was clean. The silence was broken by Ntege in his characteristic detached style. Without turning around to address anyone in particular, he asked, "I suppose you guys have heard that Entebbe Grade A has finally been annexed to State House?" Silence. "All the health workers there are being moved to Grade B," he continued. Ntege had some attachment to the Entebbe hospitals, having worked at both of them sometime in his earlier years.
>
> "What do you mean, 'finally'?"
>
> "It has been long in coming."
>
> "So, one family has appropriated for themselves a hospital that served an entire district? Folks, that is not wisdom. Poor people pray. When they realize that their hospital has been taken over by a family that could see any doctor in the country without leaving their home, they will pray. Their ailments will be transferred to the new occupants of their hospital. The people in that compound will suffer from strange and extraordinary diseases." As always, Winnie saw a spiritual angle to the problem.
>
> "Of course State House is not about one family. It is an institution. If they do maintain it as a hospital it will serve many people."
>
> "Right," Winnie retorted. "It is an institution dedicated to the service of one family. The ground on which the hospital stands has not

moved. The walls of State House have moved around it. Why did they not simply create a gate in their wall allowing access to the hospital? The whole thing stinks of selfishness and a complete lack of respect for the tax payers of Wakiso district who now have to travel longer distances in search of health care. But here is the irony. The First Lady is the champion of Safe Motherhood, the Patron of the Uganda Women's Efforts to Save Orphans ... and a few other titles that speak of a commitment to improving people's health. That the First Family forcefully and violently closes the doors of a hospital in the face of the people is most bizarre. Politicians usually want to be known for building hospitals, not closing them down."

***

In 2002 the Ministry of Defense and State House commenced plans to take over Grade A Hospital, seated on 5 acres of prime land in Entebbe Municipality, Wakiso District. The news sparked resistance from Wakiso District leadership. The hospital served as the primary medical facility for more than 100,000 people, and was especially key for the care of over 4,000 patients on treatment for HIV. The district had instituted a cost-sharing scheme at the facility and significant revenues were coming into the district coffers regularly. Wakiso mounted a serious pushback, and the take-over plans seemed to have been abandoned. As it were, the tree had been cut and the stump left for dead, but the rooting system was intact. In 2011 the take-over plans resurfaced. The grab was imminent. After a series of exchanges in which it became apparent that the hospital would be taken over by the army, the district leadership staged a street demonstration as a last ditch effort against the move. The Police and army responded with tear gas and live ammunition. In the scuffle that ensued, the district chairperson was arrested and several people were injured and arrested. The unpleasant episode was widely reported in the local media, and the topic eventually came to the floor of Parliament. When the State Minister for Health, Sarah Opendi, was questioned about the hospital, first she said that she did not have sufficient information, and then contradicted herself by saying that the Ministry had no plans to give away the hospital. In a subsequent statement, she said that the government planned to turn the facility into a trauma and VIP treatment centre, which was why they were evacuating it. It was not lost on the district leadership that the take-over plans had emerged at the time that State House, whose grounds were adjacent to Grade A Hospital, was undergoing extensive renovation. Clearly, the intention was for the State House grounds to be extended to absorb the hospital.

The demonstrators should have saved themselves the tear gas, as the take-over plans were already in motion, well away from nosy journalists. A letter dated 22 August, 2011, and signed by the Ministry of Health's Permanent Secretary, Asuman Lukwago, instructed the hospital management to evacuate the facility and hand it over, not to State House, and not to some contractor that was going to build the trauma center, but to the UPDF Special Forces Unit. "I wish to inform you that Ministry of Health agreed to hand over Entebbe Grade A Hospital to the Special Forces at the time of completion of State House rehabilitation," the letter read in part. On the 21st of October 2011, the Permanent Secretary of the Ministry of Health called the hospital superintendent and instructed him to execute the hand-over on the 1st of November.[30]

***

That there were challenges with the delivery of medical care in the country was not news. After years of paying it only lukewarm attention, and blaming health workers for all that was wrong, in 2010 President Museveni decided to act. He created a new entity in State House, the Medicines and Health Service Delivery Monitoring Unit, and appointed his personal physician, Dr. Diana Atwine to head it.

A specialist clinician, Atwine had no known experience in the management of health services. This did not deter her from taking on her new role with missionary zeal. Despite government's perennial and severe under-investment in the system that Atwine was being asked to monitor, her office was given enough money to enable her to crisscross the country apprehending health workers, and dragging some of them into police stations for various alleged transgressions. Where the ministries of health and local government jointly charged with the quality of health care were starved of resources, and health

---

[30] Martin Ssebuyira. State House takes Entebbe Hospital. The Monitor 28 August 2011.

workers were going for months without pay, Atwine's outfit had offices and staff, vehicles and drivers. The Ministry of Health had a Department of Quality Assurance whose mandate Atwine now appeared to take over. She was media savvy. In one dramatic appearance before the Parliamentary Health Committee, Atwine gave a riveting account of a collapsed health care system[31]: "In Kamuli [hospital], a brand new X-ray machine has been kept in a box for the last 12 years. In Kyanamukaka, Masaka, the hospital staff turned the [operating] theater into a store [for sorghum]. In Masindi, two doctors had all the facilities [they needed] but could not operate on patients because they didn't know how it is done."

The revelations went on and on. "… sixty per cent of the facilities visited had expired drugs, 69 per cent of the managers of government hospitals were absent, the patients were being treated by [only] junior doctors. … Then there is the problem of forged accountability. This is an everyday activity. Everywhere I go, people are stealing money and [giving] false accounting. The biggest problem is extortion right from Mulago National Referral Hospital to the lower units. Most health facilities we visited were non-functional yet they had all the facilities, including theaters. In Jinja Hospital, interns extort money openly and it is acceptable. The issue is not [lack of] money; it is the uncoordinated activities, negligence and wastage in the system. We are the problem."

The media loved it. The Ministry of Health officials were squirming in their seats. A section of the medical fraternity were skeptical of Atwine's work methods, and many were outright upset. If she wanted to help them, why was she not telling the country how poorly paid the medical workers were, or how ill equipped most facilities were?

It would not be long before the tables turned, and the watchdog became the provider. Then Atwine would have the opportunity to rectify all the ills she had identified in the system.

***

---

[31] Yasiin Mugerwa. State House gives MPs hospitals rot evidence. *The Monitor*. 5 April 2016

The Patient

The cafeteria on the sixth floor of Mulago Hospital next to the Interns' Mess had become popular as a lunchtime meeting place. Senior House Officers had their meals here, and it was an opportunity to catch up with friends, and to find out what was going on in the hospital beyond one's immediate responsibilities. It was probably the only time different disciplines sat together in one place. Most conversations were related to patients and the welfare of the doctors, but occasionally the discussion turned to politics. The subject turned to the difficulties of getting home late at night for doctors on call.

"Amin had solved that problem. He gave all doctors from the registrar up personal cars."

'True. And then he made the country so insecure that the doctors could not drive the cars at night! He gave with one hand and took away with the other."

"Obote did not give doctors any cars, but most doctors seemed to have fared well, at least during Obote I. The medical facilities were better. And the doctors had decent accommodation close to the hospital. I understand that the facility on Yusuf Lule Road now occupied by the Chieftaincy of Military Intelligence[32] (CMI) used to belong to Mulago. Museveni took doctors' houses and gave them to spies."

"Well, Obote and Amin actually used the services of this hospital. Obote was operated here. He was not afraid to go under anesthesia in Mulago." Okurut was finishing his specialist training in anaesthesia.

"Why would he fear? Surgeons are not assassins. One does not go to school for decades and swear oaths like we do to become an assassin. For that, one learns how to shoot a gun. I don't know how long it takes to become an expert marksman, but it certainly takes a whole

---

[32] The headquarters of the Chieftaincy of Military Intelligence (CMI) are located on Yusuf Lule Road, across the road from the New Mulago Hospital main gate. The facility that CMI occupies was Mulago Hospital doctors' housing, and was perfectly located for easy access to the hospital at all hours.

lot more skill to repair the human body than to make a hole in it." Baka had no Bible verse to back up his claim.

"So much for your vain skill," Babumba retorted. He mostly listened, but whenever he spoke, his skepticism and frustration were just beneath the surface. "We are talking about the destiny of a nation. Here was a man who was poised to plunge the country into the abyss, and who indeed did, and all you can say is that the surgeons of the day exercised their skill? Nobody was asking them to be serial killers. They could have taken out just the one man."

"One man? Is it ever just one man? If you think by putting one man out of action, no matter how evil you might perceive him to be, that you would prevent the country from going down the abyss as you say, then you are even more naïve than I thought. During the Roman occupation of Israel, high priest Caiaphas thought the same. He is reported to have famously said of Jesus the Nazarene, that it was better for one man to die, than for the entire nation of Israel to be destroyed.[33] They arrested Jesus and hanged him after a kangaroo court found him guilty of, of all things, equating himself to God.[34] More than two thousand years later, we are still dealing with the fallout of that ill-advised crucifixion. So – we might have suffered under Obote, but there is no guarantee that we would have fared better had he been assassinated back then. All I can say is that to his credit, he had invested in the health service enough that when he needed an emergency operation he could find it in the local hospital. Mulago had decent infrastructure for its day, and it boasted of well trained professional staff; that is what saved his skin. Or rather, his jaw and his life."

That sounded like a good point on which to end the debate, as the cafeteria staff were impatiently waiting to clear the tables.

***

---

[33] The Bible, The Gospel according to John 11:49-50
[34] The Bible, The Gospel according to John 5: 18; Acts of the Apostles 13:28-30

"Today I had the privilege of witnessing the First Lady's convoy pushing a hoard of school children into a trench. It was quite impressive." Francis sounded unusually upbeat.

"Hmm … What is impressive about that?" Karungi was only half listening, her attention on something she was reading.

"Well – for starters, the good lady needs no less than fourteen vehicles to get around. The thirteenth is an ambulance and the fourteenth is the infamous toilet on wheels. She will not be counted among the 32% Ugandans with no access to a latrine. And if you are familiar with Gadhafi Road as it plunges into the valley from Makerere Hill road, you will know why the kids had to dive into the trench. That road is a death trap for pedestrians."

"Her fuel bill must be something to behold. We had better hurry up and get that oil flowing."

"Funny, that the First family is moving around in huge convoys that include ambulances, and they have found it necessary to annex a whole hospital to State House. Someone needs to tell them the folly of what they are doing. If something were to happen to one of them, and they needed a lifesaving procedure, do they really believe that their army of handlers could stop that convoy, safely move the patient into the ambulance, stabilize them, and then airlift them to Germany for the procedure? A death certificate is final; it does not matter where it is written."

"If I were the President or the First Lady I would always travel in the ambulance itself." Ntege had not even turned around. It sounded as though he was talking to his book in the corner.

***

The Monday morning departmental meeting was over. There had been one main agenda item – the shortage of surgical sutures. For weeks now some surgical procedures had been put off, or had been done with substandard sutures. Reports from Obstetrics said that mothers going for caesarian section were buying their own sutures on the open market. In some cases, the results were catastrophic. The Hospital Director had issued instructions that no doctor should ask a patient to buy sutures. It was a tough choice – use what there was or stay out of theatre. There was only one type of suture, mostly used in children or on delicate tissues. It was inappropriate for most adult surgery. The meeting ended without any solution, and the Head of Department promised to revisit the matter with the Hospital Director. Surgeons started to disperse. Ntege had an outpatient clinic to run, but it never really got started any earlier than 9.00AM because of the time it took for the records clerks to get all the files organized, and the patients sorted out. There was no rush. He was beginning to turn away from the table when a headline on the *Monitor* in the middle of the table caught his attention. 'Uganda government takes Sh 1.7 trillion for jet fighters.'[35]

"Wait! Is this today's?"

"Yes, the paper is today's. But it is old news. From the story, the money was taken a while back, and the purchase is only now coming to light," volunteered Francis.

"US$720 million. That is serious money."

"Yup! We could be swimming in top notch sutures forever," offered one of the surgeons who had been listening in.

"We could be swimming in better salaries too," added Karungi. Then as an afterthought, "but what if we got attacked by the Russians? It has not happened since Uganda came into being, but hey, there is always a first time."

"Right! Come to think of it, if we do not have sutures, some patients will die. On the other hand, if we do not have fighter jets, this whole enterprise called Uganda could be brought to an abrupt end!" Francis no longer laughed at his own cynical jokes.

---

[35] Yasiin Mugerwa. Uganda Government takes Sh1.7 trillion for jet fighters. The Monitor, 27 March 2011.

In April 2010, as the country readied itself for the general elections, a leading Russian business daily, *Vedomosti*, reported that Uganda had signed a contract with Moscow to buy SU-30-MK2s fighter jets at Shs654 billion (US$315 million). When asked about the purchase, the army spokesperson denied the reports. At the height of the campaigns for the February 2011 general elections though, President Museveni asked Parliament to approve an emergency supplementary budget of Shs600 billion (US$253 million) from the Central Bank. It was labelled a classified expenditure, putting it beyond scrutiny. On 23 March 2011, a month after the election, President Museveni invited the Members of Parliament belonging to the ruling NRM party to State House for a nighttime meeting. The agenda was not disclosed until the meeting commenced. The President told the MPs that government needed US$740 million (about Shs1.7 trillion) from Bank of Uganda to buy fighter jets and other military hardware. He said the country needed to acquire the jets and other equipment to beef up the capacity of the UPDF. On inquiring about the urgency, and why it could not simply be put into the budget for the following year, it turned out that the money had in fact already been spent, and the Executive would be asking the Parliament to approve it retrospectively. "The President told us that the money was used to buy fighter jets and other military hardware he didn't name. He said he wanted us to approve a retrospective supplementary of US$740m obtained from the Central Bank," one of the MPs later told the press on condition of anonymity. Because military purchases were considered classified, it was not possible, either before or after the purchases, for Parliament to verify them. For the total approved annual budget, the Shs1.7 trillion was equivalent to the infrastructure and health budgets combined. The budget performance report for the financial year 2010/11[36] showed that Security and State House supplemental budgets increased the budget by 30%.

---

[36] Annual Budget Performance Report FY2010/11, Ministry of Finance, Planning, and Economic Development. October 2011.

> Each of the two supplemental budgets (Shs600 billion and Shs. 1.7 trillion) far exceeded the 3% limit stated in Section 12(1) of the Budget Act 2001, this being supplementary expenditure for which the Executive can seek retrospective authority from Parliament. The anomaly had no precedent in the history of the legislative body.

**

On 14 April 2011, casualties began to arrive at the Accident & Emergency around 11.00am. Dr. Wangoda had heard that there were confrontations between the Police and opposition politicians and their supporters over walk-to-work demonstrations.[37] They were supposed to be peaceful but they had turned violent after the Police attacked the peaceful demonstrators. One of the first patients to arrive was a nurse.

"I was walking to work when the Police started to throw tear gas canisters at people in front of me …"

The intern doctor interrupted her. "Why do you people involve yourselves in these things?"

"I was not involved. I was walking to work …"

"Precisely! Did you not hear the Police warning that anyone engaged in walk-to-work demonstrations would be arrested?

"But doctor, how were people who usually walk to work supposed to get there today?" the now agitated patient asked. "Will the Police transport us to work?"

"Oh. Do you mean to say you were walking to work …?"

"Yes. That is what I have been trying to say. I live in Nangabo and work at the Kasangati Health Center. I was approaching the Health Center

---

[37] Gillian Nantume. Walk-to-Work: Eye witnesses narrate how chaos unfolded. The Monitor 1 May 2018.

entrance when the Police threw tear gas canisters at the people ahead of me. I saw a pregnant woman drop to the ground. I rushed to help her up. One of the policemen ran to where we were and started to hit both of us. I managed to drag the woman towards the Red Cross ambulance that was parked close by. I was helping her into the vehicle when I felt something hit me in the leg. A severe pain shot up and down my leg and I felt the leg give way under me. I collapsed and half rolled under the ambulance. When I looked down at my leg, it was bleeding. A Red Cross volunteer pulled me into the ambulance."

The patients kept coming. Most of them were brought by the Red Cross ambulances, but some came on Police Patrol pick-up trucks. With the arrival of the patients came journalists and various types of security personnel, some overt and others covert. By afternoon the Accident & Emergency department looked like a field hospital in a war zone. In addition to the many demonstrators who had been assaulted by the Police, there were patients from the health center who suffered acute exposure to tear gas. More than twenty school children from a roadside school were coughing and hysterical after a couple of canisters exploded in their classroom. A pregnant woman delivered in one of the Red Cross ambulances, and the procedure was completed by one of the A&E nurses with the ambulance parked outside the Accident & Emergency Department.

At Kasangati the ambulance driver was beginning to ease the vehicle out of the roadside spot where he and the crew had been waiting for casualties when a part of the crowd of demonstrators started running towards him. They were half dragging and half carrying someone in a checked blue and white shirt. The driver put on his brakes and waited. The air was thick with dust and tear gas. One of the Red Cross volunteers opened the ambulance door and jumped out. As the men got closer the driver could see who the casualty was – Dr. Kizza Besigye, opposition leader and champion of the walk-to-work demonstrations. He was covered in dirt from head to toe and bleeding from his hands, which he held close to his chest. There were already three injured young men on board but there was certainly room enough for the man at the center of the demonstrations. As soon as he got in the First Aider banged the door and the ambulance shot off in the direction of the city. The driver and crew were accustomed to violent confrontations between demonstrators and the security forces, but this was special. The ambulance found itself in the heart of a motorcade of heavily armed security vehicles with a *mamba* in the rear, and they were keeping up with the ambulance's speed. As they approached Mulago Hospital, Besigye, who had been quiet suddenly spoke up. "I am not going to Mulago."

"That is where we take all the patients."

"I am not going to Mulago." He repeated the statement matter-of-factly, raising neither his voice nor his blood soaked hands. For someone that had just been shot, he kept his composure. "Please take me to Kampala Hospital."

The driver up front either did not hear, or ignored the request. Soon he pulled up at the Mulago Hospital Casualty Department entrance with the Police patrol trucks in tow. The other patients were taken out of the vehicle. Besigye did not budge.

"Let's go to Kampala Hospital," the First Aider said, as he banged the door closed.

Kampala Hospital was under siege. There was a close-knit ring of soldiers around the perimeter, and they were not being subtle. There were more soldiers in the parking lot and in the corridors. Besigye was moved from the ambulance onto a trolley and straight to a resuscitation area where he could be examined and emergency care commenced. The entrance to the room was guarded by security operatives despite protestations from the hospital staff that they were interfering with the patient's right to privacy and the health workers' free movement. The subsequent trips to the X-ray department and the operating room were likewise closely guarded. For a patient that had come to the hospital of his own volition aboard an ambulance, Besigye ended up in some form of custody within the private facility. Some health workers later revealed that soldiers were inquiring into the nature of the injuries, and what the likely outcomes might be. They wanted to know the identity of the surgeons in the operating room,

The Patient

reminiscent of the Idi Amin days when doctors were killed or had to flee the country for doing their work.

***

The Department of Medicine's PG room was quiet. There was a curious writing on the flipchart at the front of the room:

On 12 May 2011 the following will happen:

1. 20 Ugandan women will die of pregnancy related conditions
2. One third of all Ugandan children below 5 years will go to bed hungry.
3. One half of all children under 5 years will be malnourished, and one-third of them (2.4 million) will be stunted.
4. 200 Ugandan children will die of malaria, pneumonia, diarrhea, malnutrition, or other preventable childhood illnesses
5. Millions of young Ugandans will roam the streets and villages in search of jobs, but they will not find them
6. More than half of Uganda's 20 million children will be living in poverty
7. State House, the official residence of the First family, will spend UGX164 millions on food and drinks
8. Mr. Museveni will be sworn in as President for the fifth time. The event will cost Ugandan tax payers 3.3 billion shillings.

Is this what you voted for?

"There must be something in the water at State House. Every occupant of that address for the last 30 years seems to have had mental health problems," Agaba commented.

"What do you mean, the last 30 years? There has been only one occupant in that period."

"Exactly my point. Even if someone was mentally very robust, if you put them in State House and President's Office, where they have a sea of praise singers, unlimited power over the country's tools of violence, unfettered access to national resources, and if this goes on for more than a decade, they will begin to believe they are a special kind of being."

"Maybe they *are* a special kind of being. What is the cause, and what is the effect? I do not think ordinary individuals organize an army and fight a bush war for five years to get to power. So we started off with someone that had unusual focus on power through violence. We subjected him to extreme hero worship for a long time and we created a power monster. The tendency to split personality probably predated the bush war, and has found full expression in the current environment." In Namisi's mind the diagnosis was no longer a matter of debate.

"You base your conclusions on the study of just one individual. That is hardly credible."

"Granted. For that we would have to look elsewhere. No other Ugandan has hang on for that long. Amin used violence to get to power. His use of state power run into early opposition here and abroad because he did not take the time to co-opt enough people with sufficient greed and sophistication to keep him in power. Obote had the time, and indeed the support of enough people, but he lacked the personal discipline to keep on top of the machinery of violence. There were many reasons for his fall, but the bottle was his ultimate undoing. For a leader to drink to intoxication on a regular basis is to court disaster. Tito Okello is hardly worth mentioning. He jumped onto a run-away horse despite having zero skill in horsemanship. He was doomed from day one. So – yes, we have a small sample and we have to expand it beyond Uganda. You examine every person who has been head of state for more than 30 years in the last 60 years. They are all, without exception, greedy violent men that surrounded themselves with greedy, educated, and selfish people."[38]

In April 2012 State Minister for Finance Matia Kasaija presented Parliament with a request for supplementary funding of Shs555.78 billion (US$221.8 million) to finance 'emergency activities'. That would increase the 2012/13 budget from Shs11.4 trillion (US$4.55 billion) to Shs11.9 trillion (US$4.75 billion). There were interesting details in his request. State House was asking for an additional Shs138.1 billion (US$55 million) in "emergency" spending, more than twice what had been approved in the main budget. While this would bring the total cost of State House to 187.1 billion (US$74.7 million), the budget for health would be Ug Shs 44.2 billion (US$17.6 million), *less than one quarter of the State House budget*. Defense, which had the lion's share at Shs555.2b (US$221.5 million) would get an additional Shs43b (US$17.2 million), bringing the total to Shs598.2b (US$238.6 million). Some of the unforeseen and now emergency State House expenditures included payments for special meals and drinks, welfare and entertainment, donations, utility payments, newspapers, stationery, and the President's increased travels. It also included more than Shs500 million (US$200,000) for legal fees in a London court, where President Museveni had been sued in his private capacity for a matter not concerning affairs of the State. Opposition Members of Parliament's efforts to block the request were unsuccessful.

The President's spokesperson Tamale Mirundi said the escalation in State House spending was reasonable: "The President's activities cannot be restricted. We have a working President and he visits all parts of Uganda. Where is the wastage in the State House Budget? The money is always

---

[38] Muammar al Gaddafi, Libya, from 1969 to 2011. Paul Biya, Cameroun, In power since June 1975 (first as Prime Minister then as President). Teodoro Obiang Nguema Mbasogo, Equatorial Guinea, in power since August 1979. José Eduardo dos Santos, Angola, from September 1979 to 2017. Robert Mugabe, Zimbabwe, in power from April 1980 until November 2017. Ali Khamenei, Iran, in power since October 1981, Denis Sassou Nguesso, Republic of Congo, in power from 1979 – August 1992 (1st time) and 25 October 1997 – present (2nd time), Hun Sen, Cambodia, in power since 26 December 1984, Yoweri Museveni, Uganda, in power since January 1986. Omar al-Bashir, Sudan, in power between June 1989 and April 2019.

accounted for and this explains why the MPs approve every year. The donations are not for Europeans, they are for Ugandans."[39]

***

Nankya[40] knew the baby was due anytime now. She had been warned about having the baby without the help of a midwife, so she moved back to her mother's home which was only a short distance from a health center. And as though that move was the cue the baby needed, the following night she went into labor. She woke up the mother, and they got their neighbor who operated a *boda-boda* to take them to the health center. As it turned out, getting there was the easy part. A guard at the center led them to the maternity ward, which seemed to be the only place open at that hour. A midwife was seated at a table. She did not get up.

"Is this your first baby?"

"No. My second."

"Did you deliver the first one normally?"

"Yes."

The midwife pointed Nankya to a bed and told her to get out her 'mama kit'.

"*Mamakiti?*"

"Yes. Do you not have the mama kit?" Nankya had no idea what this was about. She had been told to bring a plastic sheet, and she had it in her bag. It was from her first baby's delivery nearly two years ago, but she had washed it thoroughly and kept it carefully, knowing it would be needed again. She reached into her bag and pulled it out, and held it up for the midwife to see. She also took out the roll of cotton wool that she had put aside for just this moment.

---

[39] Yasiim Mugerwa. Shs300b cut from health to fund defense. *The Monitor* 2 May 2013
[40] Not real name.

The Patient

"Yes, I can see the '*kaveera*'. But where is the mama kit?"

By now Nankya's contractions were getting intense, and she was having difficulty staying still. The midwife was still seated at the table, and talking loudly enough for everyone in the ward to know that she did not have the *mamakiti*, whatever that was.

"*Nyabo*! Madam! What kind of man sends his wife to the hospital to deliver without a mama kit? I am not responsible for that pregnancy! What do you expect me to use?" She got up and moved to the bottom of Nankya's bed.

She turned to Nankya's mother, who was standing at Nankya's bedside. "*Nyabo*, did your daughter not attend the antenatal clinic? Was she not told about the mama kit? You need to go and buy gloves, a razor blade, syringes, spirit, and gauze." She walked back to the table, wrote something on a piece of paper, and handed it to her with a flair of finality. There!

And with that she marched back to her table and pulled out what looked like a crotchet set, and got to work. In all this, she did not so much as put a hand on Nankya's belly, now in full riot gear. The searing pain was becoming unbearable. She felt like her lower back was being ripped apart. She was determined not to scream, but she felt a guttural sound escape from her throat, as though it was from someone else. "*Musawo nnyamba!*" "Nurse! Help!" The midwife did not leave her table. The mother stopped at the ward door very briefly, looked back at Nankya, and stepped out into the darkness. Nankya was too engrossed in her pain to think coherently about the mother now out there looking for a pharmacy in the night. After what seemed like hours of absolute hell, punctuated by wails that got weaker and weaker, Nankya suddenly felt something give way somewhere between her lower back and her pelvis. She felt a warmth spreading down her back. She managed another wail. The woman in the next bed called out to the nurse, who this time walked over, an impatient look on her face. That look changed the instant she looked at Nankya's perineum.

***

Nankya's mother found the *boda-boda* man still waiting at the gate. She asked him to take her to a drug shop. The man did not seem surprised. Maybe this happened often, that he brought patients here in the night, and ended up driving around looking to purchase medical supplies. They drove to a nursing home in the trading center. The nurses at the nursing home had most of what she needed, but she did not have enough money to buy all the items. She was going to have to wait until morning when she could borrow the rest. The first suggestion of dawn was beginning to appear when she got back to the health center. She hastened to the maternity ward. As soon as she entered the ward, she noticed that there was some kind of curtain around Nankya's bed. She thought the baby had arrived while she was gone. But as she got closer she could hear Nankya groaning. The nurse was nowhere in sight. She came closer, and put her head against a space in the curtain where she could see Nankya, and she saw that her belly was still distended, but was now covered with a green sheet that went down to her feet. She was lying on her side, and the foot of the bed was elevated. She was still wondering what all this meant when the nurse returned.

"*Nyabo*. Your daughter delayed to come to the health center, and now she has problems."

"What problems?" Nankya's mother was alarmed.

"Her waters broke, and the baby's arm came out. She cannot push the baby. She needs to have an operation to remove the baby. But here at the health center we do not do operations. She must go to Masaka Hospital immediately."

Nankya's mother felt a wave of panic wash over her. Masaka! How were they going to get there? Was her daughter going to survive? What about the baby? She had heard of stories from Masaka Hospital, and most of them were not good. The midwife had returned to her place at the table.

"How are we going to get to Masaka?"

The Patient

"I am trying to get the ambulance. It had a problem last week but I heard that it was fixed. If it is able to move, you will have to pay the driver and buy fuel. The guard has gone to call the driver."

"Pay the driver. Buy fuel…" Even if the vehicle was available, they might not go. What money she had was already spent on buying gloves and other supplies. Fuel was not something she had ever had any reason to buy. How much would it cost?

The night nurse completed her shift and left as soon as the day staff showed up. In her hand-over she told the day nurse that the ambulance driver had not come and the patient was weak. If the driver could be found, they then needed to contact the health center In-Charge, who was the only official able to approve a trip for a patient that did not have any money. By this time Nankya was barely able to talk. She was lying in a pool of amniotic fluid mixed with blood. The intermittent labor pains that had intensified with every contraction had given way to a continuous pain that seemed to involve every fiber of her body below the umbilicus. Her breath was labored and her thoughts were getting wooly. The mother sat on a little mat by her side and periodically wiped the cold sweat off her forehead.

***

Nassali, a surgeon in Nsambya Hospital, was asked to review a patient that came through the annual medical camp at the Kampala Baptist Church. What had started as a small clinic that run in the back rooms of the church a stone's throw away from the university hospital had grown into a huge medical fair that saw close to 2,000 patients treated within the church premises in five days. Patients that needed surgical procedures would then be referred to hospitals where specialists willing to take on those patients treated them free as a service to the church. It was through this arrangement that Nassali saw the small woman that looked older than her 28 years. The referral note said she had an incisional hernia – a previous operation had left a weakness in the abdominal wall through which some of the abdominal contents would escape, to remain covered by a layer of superficial tissues and skin. She asked the woman to show her the hernia. The patient removed three layers of clothing before carefully unwrapping the fourth and last layer, a wide band that she had held in place by some safety pins. Finally, once the band was off, Nassali saw the woman's bowels descend to hang like a bag of skin over her pubis. She had seen some ugly hernias, but this was something to behold. Clearly, there were no abdominal muscles to hold the abdominal contents in place. No wonder she was so thin, the poor woman was probably afraid to eat.

"What happened?"

"I had an operation to remove a baby. The doctors said that the uterus had ruptured and was infected. I was very sick, and they had to remove the uterus to save my life. The baby was dead. I was in hospital for a month after that. The wound would not heal. I had three surgeries to try to close it but it always gave way. My mother heard about the camp and said I must come. We prayed. I know you will help me."

"Was that your first pregnancy?"

"No. My second. I have a five year old daughter."

"Sounds like you are lucky."

Nankya looked down at the bag of intestines on her lap. "Lucky? How is this lucky?"

"Yes. You could have died. You are alive. Your mother still has you. Your child is not an orphan. You are lucky."

Nankya held back the tears. The three years since the operation had been hell. Her husband had left her in hospital once her uterus was removed, and he never returned to see if she had survived. She had moved back to her mother's house, where her daughter had been living since before the operation. She had made numerous visits to different hospitals to try to find a doctor that would agree to restore her belly to its normal state, but she had been unsuccessful. One doctor had told her that they would need an artificial fabric to replace the muscles that were destroyed by the sepsis. The fabric was expensive, and not all hospitals had it. Nankya was now

The Patient

waiting to hear if this doctor would have the same story. She was hopeful though, because her mother had prayed, and told her that this trip would be different.

"Your God must have heard," Nassali said, half laughing. A visiting professor had left her some mesh, and none of her patients had needed it so far. This one was definitely going to need a lot of mesh. "You better tell your mother to pray for a patient anesthetist."

***

> 'The situation of maternal health and women's survival in Africa remains a cause for concern. You have heard for yourselves from those who have spoken before me of the dire situation and plight of Africa's women. Here in Uganda, I have spoken on many occasions about the need for zero-tolerance of maternal deaths. I know the Government of Uganda is doing everything it can, as a nation, to ensure that women do not die in pregnancy and childbirth, so needlessly.'
>
> *Hon. Janet K. Museveni, M.P., Uganda's First Lady and Minister for Karamoja Affairs at the Africa Regional Consultation on Achieving MDG 5 (Improving maternal health) at Speke Resort Munyonyo, Kampala March 27, 2012*

***

Kweete's fiftieth birthday would have passed unacknowledged, as had so many others before it, had she not returned to Mulago during the same week for her quarterly review. She arrived at the Medical Outpatient Department to find the doctors and nurses talking about 'Mulago at 50' celebrations. When she mentioned to the doctor that she was fifty herself, the doctor good-naturedly wished her a happy birthday, and added that he hoped she had been cared for better than the hospital. "If this building had been a person they would have been long dead from neglect. Poorly fed, poorly cleaned, rarely dressed, overused, and ignored when ailing. As for the plumbing and water supply, this hospital would have had recurrent strokes. It is amazing that it is still here doing a good job." The doctor motioned to Kweete to get onto the examination couch. "So – let us see how your 50 year-old heart is doing."

***

The boardroom adjacent to the Hospital Director's office was a hub of activity. The heads of all departments were meeting over the hospital's fiftieth anniversary celebrations due in October 2012. Many activities were planned for 'Mulago at Fifty.' There were the inevitable speeches, a tour of the hospital by some high level delegation, awards to good performers among the staff, and a party of sorts. Departments had submitted their wish lists. The Accident & Emergency Department's list had the usual items – a new suction machine, blood pressure machines, new trolleys, and new bed screens. But the list also contained some ambitious ideas for good measure: a patient monitor and ventilator. The Head of Department was laughed out of the meeting.

***

THE TOTTERING TEENS

'The state must be cognizant of the need for the services to be maintained. They like to say that the medical profession is a calling, but there is no calling without survival. Even a priest in the church passes a basket round to collect for his survival.' Paul D'Arbela, Ugandan professor of cardiology.

Kweete's brother Kwesi walked from Mulago to Wandegeya, a short 15 minute walk in the intense sun. The place had changed somewhat since the last time he was there, some ten years back. The corner gas station was now under a different name, and the round-about had been replaced by a complex junction whose lights seemed to be on holiday. The old market was gone, and in its place was a storied structure that housed a newer version of the market, and a host of newer businesses. Wandegeya still maintained its seedy look though. The sidewalks were very uneven, there were open sewers within spitting distance of the many eateries that characterized the place, and where there was no pavement one had to walk on the road itself and risk being run over by speeding cars. The low brick barriers meant to separate pedestrian space from motorized traffic were crumbling. The buildings were a uniform dirty brown from the dust. On his way to Friecca Pharmacy, he weaved his way around fruit sellers with their fruit piled on the pavement. Passion fruit, sour oranges, mangoes, giant avocados, tangerines. As he entered the pharmacy, it occurred to Kwesi that one probably got more health benefits from the fruit spread out on the ground than from the medications sold inside the pharmacy.

Friecca pharmacy was doing brisk business. The long window at which customers presented their prescriptions was staffed by no less than five people, presumably all pharmacists - a far cry from the Mulago hospital pharmacies where a lone pharmacist or dispenser struggled to attend to the throngs of people waiting for medicines. Kwesi presented the prescription. The pharmacist informed him that there were three different brands of the same medicine. "Which one do you want?"

"How different are they?" he asked.

"We have an Indian brand, a German brand, and one from Israel. Different prices." On further inquiry, it turned out the German brand, which the pharmacist said was the 'original', cost ten times the Indian brand, and the Israeli one was somewhere in between. The pharmacist assured Kwesi that the Indian brand was a good one as well, but was quick to add that most doctors preferred the German one. "To take no chances...", he added. Kwesi decided that the Israeli one was probably just as good, and the pharmacist was happy with his choice.

Buying medicines, especially for treating critically ill patients, was a dicey affair. Even for a doctor or pharmacist, it seemed that the transaction was based on chance and not expertise. For the non-medical the purchase was as good as buying a black box – one had no clue what they are buying.

As he walked out of the pharmacy with the medicine package in hand, he wondered as he had done many times before, why these choices were left to patients and their relatives. He had once mentioned his concerns to his cousin Karungi. Instead of allaying his anxiety though, she had made it worse.

"Yeah," she had said. "There is nothing in the looks of the packaging, or the label, or the shop from which you buy it, that guarantees you that the medicine is going to do what the doctor says it should do. In Uganda there is no guarantee that the medicine in the package matches the name on the package, and in the indicated strength. Sometimes the only way you find out is by noticing improvement once the patient starts taking the medicine. But what if they get worse? Fake medicine? Wrong diagnosis? Disease process too advanced for the medicine? None of these things are easy to decipher, especially for the medically naïve."

"Medically naïve! That is me for sure." Kwesi had managed to interject, before Karungi carried on with her ranting. Clearly, this was one of her peeves with the medical system.

"The counterfeiting industry is alive and well, and the reason there is a National Drug Authority, in addition to the National Bureau of Standards, is so that Ugandans do not have to be their own pharmaceutical watchdogs. Citizens trust that these gate-keeper agencies will ensure that only safe and effective medicines are sold in the pharmacies. It is an entirely reasonable expectation that if a qualified doctor has prescribed some medicine, and it is dispensed by a licensed pharmacy, that medicine is good for the patient. The reality is very different. People that can barely read their own language, let alone English and Latin, are shopping for the prescribed medicines and medical supplies the same way they shop for clothes. Imported is better, and if it is cheap that is wonderful. Then there are the usual name-brand shoppers who think the more expensive a commodity is the better. The prescriptions range from over-the-counter cough syrups to potent broad-spectrum antibiotics, to steroids, all the way to anti-cancer drugs that are given only by injection. Patients are shopping for catheters (specially crafted pieces of tubing used in various medical procedures), surgical gloves, syringes, surgical sutures, and specialized wound dressings. To compound the problem, the language on the medicine or equipment packaging might be Chinese, Dutch, Arabic, German, or some other language not in use in Uganda. How do these commodities find their way onto the Ugandan market? They are not sold on the black market in some back street illegal clinic. They are displayed on the shelves of clearly sign-posted and brightly lit pharmacies on the main street, waiting for the first National Drug Authority official that cares to come in and ask. One has to assume that the government has approved them for sale and consumption by the uninformed and vulnerable public."

After that Kwesi never mentioned the medicines issue to Karungi again.

On his return from the pharmacy he noticed that the lady who had come the previous night, and who seemed to be doing very poorly in the morning, had been moved close to the nurses' station. There was an attempt at privacy - a bed sheet hung on a metal frame that used to be a hospital screen. The patient still had two intravenous lines, and a tube running from somewhere under her armpit into a huge bottle on the floor. Kwesi remembered hearing that she was to be moved to the Intensive Care Unit. Clearly that had not happened. Maybe there were no ICU beds. It seemed that a patient had to be literally dying before a bed would be made available in ICU. No wonder the place had such a dismal reputation.

***

Prof. Paul D'Arbela could not resist a visit to the Department of Medicine. He had spent some of his best years here, first as a young doctor, and later as a specialist physician and head of department. The exterior did not look any different from what he recalled those many years ago. But as soon as he walked through the entrance, he knew this was a very different place. The terrazzo floor was rough and dirty. The varnish on the doors was peeling. He turned right and looked in on the room that was occupied by the graduate students in his time. It was empty. He knocked on a couple of doors and was met with silence. Finally, he turned around and made his way to the corner office that he had occupied as Head. A secretary sat behind a desk just outside the Head's office. She seemed to be the only person in the department. "Is the Head of Department in?"

"No. He has left."

"Are any of the consultants in?"

The Patient

"No. You have to come back in the morning."

D'Arbela walked out. There was a sadness around the place. This was 2013, and he knew that many senior doctors were spending more and more time in their private clinics. He had heard that grand rounds were no more, and that bedside teachings were hard to conduct because of the sheer numbers of students, and the congestion on the wards. Yet he found a deserted department at 3.00pm on a Monday very disturbing. Had he been in the hospital Senior Management Meeting a few hours earlier, D'Arbela would have understood why the once vibrant department resembled a ghost town.

***

The Senior Management Meeting ended without much accomplished. The hospital was cash-strapped and the department heads had expected some relief from the Director's communication. He started by announcing that the hospital budget had been cut even further. At first, it sounded like a joke in poor taste, but he assured the meeting that it was true. The Director explained that Mulago was one of the several institutions to be affected by new budget cuts, and was set to lose UGX5.3 billion (US$2 million). Others included the National Medical Stores and most regional referral hospitals. As they came to learn, part of the money was to be used to refund some UGX46 billion (US$17.7 million) donor money that was stolen from the Office of the Prime Minister. The rest was going to finance the ballooning expenses of State House. Reports from the different departments were a litany of complaints. The labs had put up a list of tests that could not be done because there were no reagents. The pharmacy was rationing intravenous fluids, and the list of drugs that were out of stock had become longer. The laundry unit was down to only two old machines where there should have been eight. The technicians said the machines were too old to be repaired. The surgical directorate with the operating theaters had the most complaints. Operations were being canceled because of oxygen shortages, inadequate linen, and not enough anesthetists. In the Accident & Emergency department, patients had to buy their own anesthetic drugs in order to get operated in a timely manner. The shortage of gauze and surgical sutures was perennial and was not discussed much. The meeting ended with little resolved.

***

> Uganda's per capita (per person) spending on health amounted to less than US$2 per year for most of the 1980s. In 1989 the government allocated more money to social services generally, US$63 million, equal to 26% of its development budget, and US$24 million of this allocation went to health. This represented an increase of 50 percent over health spending for the previous year. In subsequent years the actual amounts stagnated again, and the share of the national budget going to health went down. A big proportion of the health budget continued to be paid by donors. In financial year (FY) 2011/2012, donor funding totaled US$ 83.3 million, and in 2012/13, it was US$ 82.2 million.
>
> In 2012, Uganda's major donors cut aid to express their displeasure following a multi-million dollar financial scandal in the Office of the Prime Minister. Some donors demanded that the stolen money be refunded. The government undertook to refund the money rather than recover it from the OPM employees who were responsible for the losses. The donor cuts and demands from State House for supplementary spending precipitated cuts in the budgets of some sectors, key of these health, education, agriculture and water. In particular, money meant for the purchase of essential medicines, and for running hospitals, was instead diverted to State House and Defense. Mulago and regional referral hospitals were among the worst hit by the budget cuts., [41] [42]

---

[41] Yasiin Mugerwa. Sh. 300 billion cut from Health to fund Defense. The Monitor 2 May 2013.
[42] Uganda Radio Network, https://ugandaradionetwork.com/story/govt-proposes-budget-cuts-for-ministry-of-health published 8 May 2012, accessed 19 June 2019

By 2017 the government was contributing only 17% to the healthcare costs of citizens. Donors contributed 41% and individuals covered the biggest part, 42%. Under the 5-year Health Sector Development Plan (2015/16 - 2020/21), for government to meet the country's basic health needs, it needed to invest Shs3.4 billion into the sector, and to then bump it up to 3.5 billion in FY 2018/19. The government would have to spend US$91 (UGX320,000) per person on health in 2017/18 and US$96.6 in 2019/20. Instead, in the FY2017/18, the government proposed to spend around US$10 (Shs34,000) on the health of each of the 34.6 million Ugandans.

The government allocated nearly Shs1.3 trillion, or 6.9% of the total budget, to the health sector. The funding would fall far short of the Shs100, 000 (US$28) that government had set as its target health expenditure per person in the Health Sector Strategic Investment Plan. This target itself fell far short of the WHO recommendation of US$86 per person per year.[43] In 2017/2018, amidst health worker strikes for poor pay and deplorable working conditions, frequent cholera, meningitis, yellow fever, and Ebola epidemics, and a high maternal mortality that continued undented, the health share of the budget fell farther to 6.7%. *Sources: National Budget Frame Work Paper 2015, Budget speech 2015/2016, Health Sector Development Plan 2015/16 – 2019/20. Annual Health Sector Performance Reports 2015, 2016, 2017, The Monitor, May 2, 2013.*

***

Karungi walked into the boardroom and found Francis laughing. At first she thought he was on the phone, but on coming closer realized that he was not. He seemed to be talking to himself while looking at a copy of *The Monitor*. He looked up, and by way of explanation said,

---

[43] Jowett M, Brunal MP, Flores G, Cylus J. Spending targets for health: no magic number. Geneva: World Health Organization; 2016 (WHO/HIS/HGF/HFWorkingPaper/16.1; Health Financing Working Paper No. 1); http://apps.who.int/iris/bitstream/10665/250048/1/WHO-HIS-HGFHFWorkingPaper-16.1-eng.pdf

"They are going after the secondaries. They say health workers are corrupt. That they are stealing drugs and charging patients illegally. Now two nurses have been arrested at a health center in Mubende district. They were found selling a few doses of antimalarials to patients at the health center."

"And how is that funny?"

"Actually, it is not funny at all. Think about this." Now he was serious. "A nurse earns US$115 a month, but even that has not come for the last three months. She has a family. Her kids need food, school fees, clothes … where else can she find money to feed her children, but in the place where she works? Now the poor women have been arrested, humiliated, and they are being held at Mubende Police station. Their kids will starve." From laughing, he was now shouting angrily. "And you know what really gets to me? Last week a million dollars went missing from the Ministry of Health. Nobody has been arrested. That is why I say, they are going after the secondaries. The primary cancer is here at the center. It is throwing off metastases. The major thieving is being done right here. From the ministry and National Medical Stores to the local governments at the districts, to the hospitals, down to the health centers. I am surprised that by the time one gets to the health center there is anything left to steal." He was banging the desk. "So – when we deal with cancers we aim at the primary. If we can deal with the primary site early, we have a fighting chance. If we cannot find the primary site, the patient is in trouble. But here the primary site is pretty obvious. Anyone wanting to curb this vice need not leave Kampala. Why go to arrest a hungry woman in Mubende? Why?"

For Francis everything in the hospital and in the country had a parallel in cancer and its treatment. He had done his thesis on cancer of the prostate, and so that was the lens through which he saw all the country's problems. During their time as post-graduate students, the white board in the PG room was often covered with his sketches – it was never clear if he was talking about cancer of the prostate, or the dysfunction of the health care system, or indeed the corruption in the entire country. Ntege, the oldest Senior House Officer in the group, was often the sole audience for his ranting. Ntege's response was usually limited to grunts and nods, and the occasional turn of the head, but this did not discourage Francis, who would continue to expound on the inevitable consequences of the rampant corruption – once metastases established themselves in the major organs, it was impossible to kill the tumor cells without destroying the organs, and slowly but surely, multiple organ failure would set in – the liver, lungs, brain - and the end was only a matter of time. He and Karungi once had a discussion that lasted close to thirty minutes before she realized that they were not even talking about the same thing. She had come to the PG room to find Francis working on what looked like an elaborate schema for the multi-disciplinary care of the cancer patient. At the center of the board was a red circle with the word 'eradication' in bold. He had arrows pointing to different medical teams – surgeons, radiographers, physiotherapists, nutritionists, and so on. Francis presented the case.

"The diagnosis was first made in 2001. Before that there had been divided opinion. The 2001 consensus should have been the opportunity for total excision – the complete removal of the tumor, at a time when it was still localised. That opportunity was lost. The next five years saw the tumor spread rapidly and the progress was largely unchecked. The spread was typical – local, then regional, and through sending metastases to far flung organs – usually by eroding into blood vessels, so that microscopic bits of the tumor tissue were washed into the blood stream, and carried all over the body. Once this happened, total excision ceased to be an option."

Francis paused and looked at Karungi with a mixture of amusement and resignation. She was not certain whether he was expounding on the natural history of malignant tumors, or discussing his pet subject, the politics of corruption. He went on.

"In 2006 there was a spirited attempt to excise the growth. Sadly, there was poor preparation for this heroic but ill-advised plan. The patient had not been prepared for the nature and scope of the surgery. The tumor had not been 'staged' – that is, its full extent was not well appreciated. Other than the primary site, which was obvious, what other tissues were affected? Was there a clear plane between the tumor and normal tissue? What was going to be sacrificed during the excision attempt? What would the team do if the patient bled excessively during the surgery? How would the pain be controlled? If the excision were successful, how would the post-operative period be managed? There is little evidence that all this had been clearly thought through."

Francis paused again. Ntege grunted and carried on flipping through some book.

"In order to prepare for the extensive surgery, the following should have been involved, or at least considered: Radiotherapy. It limits the growth, can effectively shrink the tumor, and make excision possible. But it leaves healthy tissues damaged, and depresses the patient's immunity.

"Chemotherapy kills tumor cells wherever in the body they are found. But it kills lots of normal cells as well, and leaves the body's immunity in tatters. It must be used with caution. The patient could have used some psychotherapy. There is little evidence that these modes of treatment were used in preparation for the 2006 surgery.

"The surgical team was determined and well intentioned, but they lacked the necessary diagnostics. Without these services, the team was groping in the dark. They needed to know when to start the medications, when to stop or reduce doses, if they needed to give blood transfusion, and so many other actions that would have been blind without the diagnostic services. And all the above needed to be neatly tied together by solid cancer management – harnessing the resources, taking care of the finances, procuring the right medicines, ensuring the right personnel, and coordinating activities between the OR and other facilities.

"With most of these missing, the population was shocked that the treatment failed. The tumour remained firmly in place – bruised and bleeding, but not removed. It became clear that to dislodge it completely was no longer feasible. ..."

Francis would have gone on with his lecture, but just then, Winnie walked in and asked if anyone had a theater list onto which she could sneak a patient the following morning. The conversation changed.

Ntege was in his late forties, and had been practicing medicine in some rural hospital for close to two decades before he returned for post-graduate training. Nobody knew what got him to come back after so long. At entry, he had been familiar with most of the operations that many residents were trying to master, and always sounded bored when talking about what he was able to do. Some weekends he still traveled back to the rural hospital to do a theater list. He had been classmates with the Head of Surgery during their undergraduate years, and the latter was now a professor of surgery. He simply shrugged his shoulders when asked about the long lapse between his first degree and his current training.

***

The day after the Office of the Prime Minister scandal[44][45] broke, the board in PG room bore one bold statement: *War on Cancer!* Below it in small letters was the follow up: *The worst type of cancer is that which destroys the human soul.* In even smaller letters, right at the bottom of the board was the closing: *For this type there shall be no palliation.* Nambasi read it slowly, and would have let it drop had it

---

[44] Edward Ssekika. OPM SCANDAL: All ministries under probe. *The Observer* 16 November, 2012

[45] Lorenzo Piccio. In Uganda, donors divided on response to aid embezzlement scandal. 10 December 2012. https://www.devex.com/news/in-uganda-donors-divided-on-response-to-aid-embezzlement-scandal-79925 accessed 29 August 2019.

not been for Sekabunga, who entered a few moments later. Standing at the door, she read the statements aloud with the dramatic flair that they were meant to elicit. "Well! So, who are the soldiers in this war? The last time I checked, all of us were the walking wounded!"

"Sounds pretty grim. No palliation … I wonder why not."

"The whole point of palliation is that the sufferer should live out the rest of their days comfortable and free of pain, and that when the time comes they should go with dignity. Those suffering from the cancer of the soul should surely die slow, painful, and humiliating deaths."

"Wow! How so self-righteous!" Sekabunga drew a sad face by the statements, but left them well alone.

> In July 2014, shortly after the reading of the budget, the Minister in Charge of the Presidency laid out how the Presidency[46] planned to spend the nearly 1 trillion Uganda shillings allocated to it for the year.[47] At 6.6% of the national budget, it compared favorably with health at 7%. The Shs 961 billion (US$363 million) was more than double the amount allocated to the agricultural sector, which employed about 70 per cent of Uganda's labor force, and on average contributed about 21 percent to the GDP.
>
> - Shs 92.6bn to attend 70 planned community functions, and support to the (unspecified) needy.
> - Shs 83.4bn for security (Internal Security Organization (ISO), Co-ordination of Security Services, Uganda Media Centre, and presidential awards chancery)

---

[46] There were six departments under the presidency: Office of the President, Internal Security Organization (ISO), External Security Organization (ESO), State House, Uganda Aids Commission, and Directorate of Ethics and Integrity.
[47] Ministerial Policy Statement 2014/15, Office of the President. http://csbag.org/wp-content/uploads/2015/10/Office-of-the-President-Ministerial-policy-statement-FY2014-15.pdf accessed 18 July 2019.

- Shs 38.7bn for classified equipment and school fees for unspecified sponsored students.[48]
- Shs 27.6bn to host 60 delegations from districts.
- Shs 16.3bn for Ministry of the Presidency. (Out of the Shs 16.3bn, the Minister for the Presidency & State Minister each to get Shs 18.7m in allowances for mobile phones, Shs 379.5m in per diem and Shs 37.4m in responsibility allowances.)
- Shs 13.05bn to procure a specialized presidential vehicle at Shs 800m and Shs 5.2bn on buying 32 support vehicles. (In 2012, the President had bought two new limousines, whose cost press reports put variously at between Shs 6bn and Shs 10bn.)
- Shs 5.9bn to attend six international trade meetings and to officiate at both local and international trade-related functions.
- Shs 10.7bn for foreign visits to 20 countries, hosting 15 heads of state and attending 18 regional and international meetings.
- Shs 5.3bn to be deposited on a new presidential helicopter. (The President already owned two jets and a helicopter)
- Shs 3.58bn in wages for the presidential jet and helicopter crews
- Shs 1.4bn on a poverty alleviation project which included support to one (unspecified) scientific innovator to enhance rural transformation and promotion of value addition.

---

[48] State House scholarships have been criticized for lacking in transparency, being used as a patronage tool, and to enhance inequality. In 2012, the President announced that he was considering phasing them out in favor of the more transparent Student Loan Scheme. Rather than phase out, the scholarships kept increasing. By 2017 the demand from State House was UGX20 billion. Mrs. Museveni, the Minister of Education, told Parliament that the Student Loan Scheme would be shelved for lack of UGX5 billion.

> - Shs 53m *monthly* for presidential contributions for burial expenses
>
> The Shadow Minister for the Presidency in Parliament pointed out that a reduction by half of the President's 762 advisors could provide enough funds to recruit at least four more doctors for each of the 112 districts. The advisors took up to Shs 234.3bn annually (93.7 percent) in salaries of the State House's total allocation of Shs 249.84bn, enough to pay salaries for 16,271 junior doctors each at a monthly pay of Shs 1.2m. The same budget could pay at least 12,204 specialist doctors each a monthly salary of Shs 1.6m and 9,763 consultant doctors each at a monthly pay of Shs 2m.

***

The nurses from the Accident & Emergency department went up to Old Mulago and surveyed the space that was going to be their workspace. At that time in early 2015 they thought it would be for only a few months. It was immediately evident that this was going to be tough. If they had complained about inadequate space before, now they were going to work with far less. Nine beds was all there was. The same general areas served as both the Accident & Emergency, and the surgical emergency ward. The two well-used patient monitors that had given the High Dependence corner in the A&E a believable look were now going into storage. The sole ventilator, if it survived the move, was going to sit in a corner unused, away from the nurses' station. There were no electricity outlets into which to plug it close to the nurses' station, as the whole area had only one socket. There was no provision for piped oxygen, and for that, they were going to rely on two cylinders for the whole unit. The X-ray unit was farther up the hill, with several series of steps in between. Patients who could not walk were going to be wheeled there on their beds, which were not designed for such transfers.

The day finally came when the Accident & Emergency department had to be moved up the hill. It was moved in phases; first some beds, then the equipment, and finally the patients that remained on the ward. Everything in the new quarters was improvised, from the narrow sidewalk that served as an ambulance bay, to the stabilization and treatment cubicles, created by using curtains to partition the area.

The first full day of working in the new Accident & Emergency space confirmed everyone's fears. The area was not only very small, but the infrastructure was grossly inadequate. The patients' beds were crammed too close together, ignoring the fact that the medical workers and their trolleys needed to get to the patients. There was no easy way for the workers, patients, and their many relatives to wash their hands, or anything else, since there were no sinks. Perhaps most distressing, there was no way to remove the bodies of patients who died during the night. The best that the night staff could do was to pull out the bed and push it into a corner by the door, to await the mortuary attendants who came through in the morning. On a bad night, the corner would be too narrow for the mortuary bound beds, leaving some patients lying within a few feet of their departed neighbors.

***

On 17 December 2015, as the last units of the dilapidated New Mulago Hospital were being evacuated for renovation, His Highness Prince Karim Aga Khan IV visited Uganda as a special guest of President Museveni. In preparation for the visit, the President, and especially the then minister for Lands, Housing and Urban Development, Daudi Migereko, worked around the clock to clear and avail the Aga Khan with 60 acres of prime public land for the construction of a new teaching hospital. "*The government undertakes to waive payment of any premium for the lease or in any respect for the land,*" said the agreement. In an agreement that was supposed to remain confidential, having been written in State House, the Aga Khan Foundation would pay one hundred United States dollars (US$100) per year, a total of $10,400 (about Shs 34.3 million) to use the land for the first 104 years of its lease ($500 for the first five years and $9,900 for the next 99 years). In addition, the Aga Khan Foundation would enjoy "*exemptions of all forms of taxes, and government guarantees for foreign loan applications as follows:*

"The government acknowledges and confirms that the not-for-profit social development agencies of the Aga Khan Development Network are exempt from the payment of all taxes direct and indirect, fees, duties and imposts in accordance with the Accords and Protocols of the Cooperation for Development in Clause 2 hereof and the Statutory Instruments that have been issued by the Government of Uganda published in the Official Gazette. ...In the event that the Development Covenant has not been fulfilled by the expiry of the initial five (5) year term, it shall be extended for such further period as may be reasonably necessary (having regard to the full context and international best practice),"* said the agreement. The government of Uganda, through the Minister of Finance, Planning and Economic Development, agreed to *"provide letters in support of the project and other education and research initiatives in Kampala to international funding agencies and institutions to facilitate grants, soft loans and concessional funding for the project."* Additionally, in accordance with the standing rules on land allocation within the city, which require the government to offer an initial five years that can be extended upon fulfillment of initial development requirements, the five-year lease to the Aga Khan is supposed to automatically turn into a perpetually-renewable 99-year lease. The government was bending over backwards, and clearing every possible obstacle in the path so that the Aga Khan could enter the market and take free shots in a field where the local investors in health care and medical education were shackled with high interest loans.

On 9 October 2017, during the country's Independence celebrations, President Yoweri Museveni awarded His Highness Prince Karim Aga Khan IV, the 'Most Excellent Order of Pearl of Africa, The Grandmaster' to recognize his decades of work and contribution to Uganda's development. The Aga Khan, a British citizen, is ranked among the top ten wealthiest royals in the world.

***

In January 2016, Prof. Sewankambo stepped down from the position of Principal, Makerere University College of Health Sciences. He had led medical education at Makerere for more than two decades. He had steered the medical school through the complex process of forming a college, setting the pace for the rest of the university to adopt the college system.

First as dean of the medical school, and later as the first principal of the new College of Health Sciences, he had presided over the growth and expansion of medical education in many aspects – from research, to international collaborations and partnerships, and the introduction of many new graduate programs. Offerings had grown from one degree program – the Bachelor of Medicine and Bachelor of Surgery – to over thirty programs by 2016. It was often acknowledged that Makerere's international reputation had partly to do with the level and volume of research coming out of the college. It was rumored that despite this impressive portfolio, there were some who were impatient to see Sewankambo go, and with him some of the initiatives he had championed. Key among these programs was Problem Based Learning. A few months after his departure from office, the new administration called a senior faculty meeting at Rydar Hotel Mukono. When that meeting ended, Problem Based Learning was over. It was not immediately apparent what curriculum would take its place, but there would be plenty of time to figure that out. For now, the curriculum that some medical education gurus had said would move Makerere from good to great, and that had received a positive evaluation a few years previously[49], was retired without notice.

***

Nabulime noted that the patient reviewed by the neurosurgeon was pregnant. The woman had fallen off a *boda-boda* and sustained a head injury. The surgeon ordered for a CT scan, and the relatives left to go and find the money to pay for it. By the time they got back the radiographer had left, so the patient was wheeled back to the ward to wait for the night shift when another radiographer might be able to do the imaging. By the time the imaging was done the neurosurgeon was long gone, so the patient was admitted, to be seen in the morning when both the surgeon and the imaging results would be available. Nothing was said about the pregnancy beyond noting that the patient was indeed pregnant, at an estimated 30 weeks' gestation. As she prepared to hand over to the night shift, Nabulime

---

[49] E. Kiguli-Malwadde, S. Kijjambu, S. Kiguli, M. Galukande, A. Mwanika, S Luboga, N. Sewankambo. Problem Based Learning, curriculum development and change process at Faculty of Medicine, Makerere University, Uganda. *African Health Sciences* 2006 **6**(2): 127-130

noticed that the patient was more restless, and she thought it might be the pregnancy. On closer observation, she noted that the patient was having uterine contractions, at which point she decided that it was best to get an obstetric consultation. But the entire obstetric department had been shifted from Mulago to Kawempe Hospital, a good 3km away.

After a few frantic calls to see if a doctor in Obstetrics could come and review the patient, and discovering that this was not possible, Josephine decided that the best solution was to transfer the patient to Kawempe. But on whose orders? Technically speaking, the patient was between caregivers – she was admitted in the A&E only as accommodation to await a neurosurgeon, but now she was clearly in need of an obstetrician. An intern on call came and wrote the transfer note so that the patient could be moved to Kawempe, where a Senior House Officer promised to review her on arrival. To his credit, the Senior House Officer was waiting. He examined the patient, prescribed some medication, and instructed that the patient be returned to Mulago A&E to await the neurosurgeon.

***

> Okello sat outside the operating theater in Kawempe Hospital pondering his next move. The theater was closed following a thunderstorm which ripped part of the roof off the relatively new building that housed Mulago's newly relocated Department of Obstetrics and Gynecology. Thankfully, there were no procedures happening at the time of the storm, but it meant that the theater would be unusable until the repairs and were complete, and the flooded theater restored to sterility. The patient list was long, and some patients had been waiting for as long as three weeks on the ward. One woman with a virginal fistula had been waiting for surgery for months.
>
> Okello recalled a meeting he had attended the previous month at which Kisamba Mugerwa, chair of the National Planning Authority, talked of Uganda attaining middle-income status by 2020. Mugerwa had displayed graphs and figures that showed Uganda's aspirations, and rosy economic projections for 2040. Okello wondered if such

people ever visited places like Mulago. His musings were interrupted by another Senior House Officer, Mugisha, who came up the stairs just then.

"What is the state of our new theater? It seems to have fallen apart with the first serious downpour."

"Yeah. Brand new and leaking. We are told that Uganda is on its way to achieving middle-income status. To hear politicians tell it you would think that it is something that comes about because the President wills it. We cannot work because a storm has torn the roof off a new hospital building, and the officials at the Ministry of Health are losing no sleep over it. But somehow, almost as though it was by magic, we are still steadily marching on to middle-income status. I bet you some politicians think that Museveni is so powerful, he will simply declare Uganda middle-income and it will be so."

"Well! You sure needed to get that off your chest! Storms damage buildings the world over."

"No, really! I am sick of that song," retorted Okello. "Ugandans need to face the truth; that we are so far down the development ladder that if there was a category called 'less-than-low-income' that is where we would belong. The sight of all those obese ministers and MPs laughing at the President's stale jokes makes my stomach turn. Excuse me."

And with that he got up and headed down the stairs.

Mugisha was on call, and did not have the luxury of walking away. He had hoped that he could get some elective procedures done before the inevitable emergencies in the evening. He was going to find some way of operating, whether or not the roof was leaking.

***

Nabulime heard the wails before she saw where they were coming from. There was nothing unusual about relatives wailing when their patients died. She turned the corner to enter the Accident & Emergency Department, and met with the wailing woman. She recognized her from the previous night when the pregnant patient was returned from Kawempe. The woman had been waiting for the ambulance, and had told Josephine the patient was her sister-in-law. *"Musawo! Mwanyinazze afuuse Salongo nga taleze ku balongo! Wooweee!"* "My brother was expecting twins, but he has not had the opportunity to hold them in his arms!"

Prof. John Sebuwufu, first Ugandan professor of Anatomy.

Prof. Samuel Luboga, Anatomist, surgeon, educationist.

Dr. Matthew Lukwiya, Executive Director, St. Mary's Hospital Lacor, Gulu, 1997-2000.

Dr. Specioza Wandira Kazibwe

Prof. Nelson Sewankambo. *Monitor Publications Limited.*

Dr. Jackson Orem. (image provided by Dr. Orem)

Prof. Francis Omaswa. (image provided by Prof. Omaswa)

Prof. Alexander Odonga

***

For a very long time the Radiotherapy Department was little known to Ugandans, except those unfortunate enough to need it. The building that housed the department was tucked away in the back of the hospital, its closest neighbors being the garbage management unit and the workshop. Those were true back-end operations that should not attract the attention of the ordinary patient. Except that cancer patients were no ordinary patients. Most of them had been sick for a long time, and a good proportion of them were in all likelihood going to die from their disease – they were considered terminally ill. This grim view did not represent the full reality though, as in fact, many cancers were curable with early diagnosis and appropriate treatment. But in Mulago early diagnosis and appropriate treatment were more the exception than the rule. By April 2016 the demand for radiotherapy was so acute that patients were having to endure weeks or months of waiting after diagnosis, before they could begin treatment.

It was only 7am but the line outside the Radiotherapy Unit was already long. Many of the patients in the line were from the hostel within the hospital, but there were some that came in from outside. The nurses came early, registered the patients, and retrieved their records. The doctors and technicians moved back and forth, checking equipment and ensuring the scheduled patients had all the required tests done and documented. Then things slowed down. No patients were called. The line grew longer. There was unease. The talk in the corridor was that there was a technical problem. The accelerator would not start. This had happened a few times in the past, but the technicians had always been able to resolve the problem. By 11am word had gone round that the 'cancer machine' was not working. At noon, the doctors announced that the day's treatments were not going to happen, but they assured the patients that the following day they would be able to treat everyone. The following day the machine did not revive. By the end of the week it had become official. The old Cobalt-60 radiotherapy machine, which had served faithfully for more than two decades, had breathed its last - or rather, burnt its last - leaving thousands of patients with no effective cancer treatment. Uganda's population of close to 40 million people, with some of the highest rates of cancers worldwide, had no access to radiotherapy within their borders.

The Patient

Broken machines, broken lives. [50, 51, 52]

The Uganda Cancer Institute is the oldest such facility in East and Central Africa. Cancer treatment started as early as 1967 with the opening of the Lymphoma Treatment Center by Dr. John Ziegler and his colleagues from the USA's National Cancer Institute. For the first two and a half decades, the Institute had no radiotherapy service. In 1995 that changed. Below is the tortuous and incredible history of this cancer treatment service.

1995: A used Chinese-made Cobalt-60 machine was installed at Mulago national referral hospital. It was expected to work for 10 to 12 years at most.

2000: Efforts started to expand radiotherapy services in the country, including two more External Beam radiotherapy units at Mulago, and centers to be constructed in three regional hospitals.

2000 – 2005: No action on the expansion plans because of 'budgetary constraints', according to Ministries of Finance and Health.

2002: A major overhaul of the old machine, including the radioactive source exchange.

2005: Expansion plans were dropped altogether.

---

[50] J. B. Kigula Mugambe and P. Wegoye. Pattern and experience with cancers treated with the Chinese GWGP80 Cobalt unit at Mulago Hospital, Kampala. East Afr. Med. J. 2000; 77 (10): 523 -25.
[51] Kigula Mugambe J.B, Durosinmi- Etti F.A. Radiotherapy in cancer management at Mulago Hospital, Kampala - Uganda. East Afr. Med. J. 1996; 73: 611-613.
[52] Elmore SN, Sethi RV, Kavuma A, Kanyike DM. Broken Machines or Broken Systems: The Road to Meaningful Global Radiotherapy Access J Glob Oncol. 2016;3(5):438-440.

2008: A new plan was hatched to replace the overhauled but already malfunctioning Cobalt-60 unit. Consultations into its replacement yielded the following options: (a) Instead of buying a new machine and source, buy only a new source (of the radiation) and put it in the old machine. (b) If a disruption in radiotherapy services can be tolerated, purchase a new cobalt machine with its source and install it in the existing bunker. (c) Leave the old machine alone. Purchase a new Cobalt-60 machine with its new source, and install them in new premises. For another two years, none of the options was pursued.

2010: Mulago hospital administration identified a contractor to construct a new bunker, and to procure and install a new Cobalt-60 machine.

2011: More consultations (Frederic Johannes Lange) recommended that a bunker should be designed and constructed for expansion of radiotherapy services. Before anything happened, there was a change in Mulago Hospital administration. The new administration terminated the procurement process citing procurement irregularities.

2012 - 2013 the new administration planned relocation of the radiotherapy department, and worked in consultation with International Atomic Energy Agency on designs for new radiotherapy bunkers (2 EBRT / 1 HDR and other auxiliary facilities).

June 2013: Radiotherapy Department moved to the Uganda Cancer Institute (UCI). The UCI administration noted inaccuracies with the proposed bunker designs and halted the procurement and designing processes.

2014: Uganda Cancer Institute restarted the plan with a much bigger projection - (4 EBRT / 2 HDR and other auxiliary facilities).

> April 2016: Old Cobalt-60 machine stopped working and was irreparable. Now the entire country had no radiotherapy services. A public outcry ensued. The government said it had arranged with Kenyatta Hospital in Nairobi for the stranded patients to receive care from there. Hopes were dashed when patients wanting to pursue this avenue of care discovered that they would have to pay for their own transportation, upkeep while in Kenya, and the actual radiotherapy treatment. Few made the trip. The UCI staff did what they could to find alternative modes of treatment, but for some cancers radiotherapy was the mainstay of treatment. Many patients returned to their villages to await inevitable death.
>
> 2016: Construction process started
>
> December 2017: Radiotherapy services resumed with a new Cobalt-60 machine installed in the old bunker after 21 months of service disruption. The machine effectively restored the Radiotherapy Unit's 1995 capacity for a population that had doubled since the first installation. Prime Minister Dr. Ruhakana Rugunda officiated at the commissioning of the sole machine. It was still the only such machine in a country of over 41 million people. Elsewhere in the world, including in some East African countries, the Cobalt-60 technology was considered obsolete, and had been replaced by the safer and far more effective linear accelerator radiotherapy technology.

***

Sheila[53] debated with herself whether to tell her supervisor that she planned to apply for a job in the Middle East. She had seen the adverts on TV[54], and heard her colleagues discuss them a few times. She had been a nurse for fifteen years, and in all that time she had never got a pay raise, despite having passed her registration exams, and having gained experience in various disciplines. She had taken every opportunity to improve her skills,

---

[53] Not real name.
[54] Ephraim Kasozi. Ugandans to get 1,500 Libyan medical jobs starting tomorrow. *The Monitor.* 24 May 2017

and she now had a raft of certificates from all the workshops that she attended. She always told herself that one of them would land her a better paying job, but so far, that had not happened. Then she saw the advert. Libya was planning to recruit nurses, doctors, and other medical workers from Uganda. It was said that the pay was very good - up to USD1,000 per month for a registered nurse. The recruiting team would take care of all the travel logistics. Sheila had barely thought of anything else since she decided to apply. It sounded almost too good to be true. At night, she lay awake thinking of all the things she could do with such money. When she was younger, she had wanted to be a doctor, and only ended up in nursing school because that year the university started charging tuition, and her parents could not afford it. She did not want the same fate for her daughter, who was now in her final year in secondary school. Yet she knew that on her current salary even nursing school tuition would be a stretch. Suddenly all that could change – if she became one of the nurses selected to go to Libya.

In the end, she decided that it was best not to tell her supervisor of her plans. If she passed the interview then she would let her know. If she did not, there was no need to alert her that she was looking for alternative employment, as that would surely put a nail in any promotion prospects that might be on the horizon.

On the morning of the interview Sheila chose her clothes carefully, to portray herself as smart but not flashy; eager but not desperate. A dependable nurse. She had the originals of her nursing diploma and all her certificates. The large manila envelope was somewhat clumsy to carry so she put it in a decent looking plastic bag. Eight o'clock found her waiting with what looked like half the city outside the hotel where the interviews were to be held. Many health workers had traveled on night buses from up-country stations to attend the interviews. At 8.30am when the doors opened there was a surge towards the doors. The security officers assured everyone that the recruiters would see everyone who had been invited, and that they were using a pre-determined list, so one's place in the hall did not matter. The pushing and shoving eased up a little. As the intense crowding at the doors loosened up, Sheila's jaw dropped. Right there in the center of

The Patient

the crowd, brown manila envelope under the arm, and the usually braided grey hair now held in a tight pitch-black ponytail, was Sister Bwanika! Her first thought was, 'traitor', but then she quickly thought, 'why not?'

For as long as Sheila had been in nursing, Sister Bwanika[55] had been a senior nurse, one of those red belt officers that were more feared than loved. She had recently been rewarded with a promotion and now wore a black belt, so in fact she was not Sister anymore, but Matron. Matron Bwanika was at the rank of Principal Nursing Officer, PNO. Every nurse below that rank dreamt of becoming a PNO. It came with quite a few perks – for starters, one did not have to do the actual bedside nursing. This special class of nurses had others under them that did their bidding. Often they were in charge of entire units, and in Bwanika's case every nurse in Accident & Emergency reported to her. She got to attend Senior Management meetings with Consultants and other senior hospital managers. Surely, nobody in that position would want to go to Libya! But there was no mistaking it, there was Bwanika, elbowing her way through the crowd of mostly younger health workers, her face set, her eyes fixed at the rather distant table where the recruiters were seated. Sheila was torn between the temptation to walk over and say good morning, at least acknowledge her in some way, and the urge to ran out of there and go back to the hospital. How was she going to explain her presence here, having told Bwanika that she was attending a teacher-parent conference at her child's school? But the thought of missing out on this once-in-a-lifetime opportunity to earn a decent salary, to put her children on a sure footing, to pay for her mother's diabetes medication without borrowing … quickly pushed the very thought of fleeing out of her mind. She had done no wrong; she was going to take her chances. She would wait in a corner until her number was called out, and then she would go straight to the front.

***

---

[55] Not real name.

In 2014, Uganda had an estimated 59,000 registered health professionals for all categories, to meet the health needs of her 35.4 million people. The Ministry of Health's human resources structure had 57,700 approved posts in government facilities, of which only 69% were filled.[56] The distribution of the health workers was far from ideal, with the majority of the health workers in urban areas despite a much larger rural population. The country had a ratio of one doctor for every 10,000 people, and one nurse for every 11,000 people.[57] The World Health Organization recommendation was for one health worker (doctor, nurse, or midwife) for every 435 people. Uganda was by World Health Organization standards a country with a severe health workforce crisis[58, 59]. Not only were the publically employed health workers far too few, but for the profession they were among the worst paid in the East African region.

In mid-2014 the Ugandan government, through its Ministry of Foreign Affairs, received a request from the government of Trinidad and Tobago for some 263 medical workers to go and work in the Caribbean country, to help improve the medical services there. An inter-ministerial committee was formed involving three ministries: Foreign Affairs, Health, and Gender, Labour, and Social Development. The Ministry of Health, acting as a recruitment agency for Trinidad & Tobago, put out a call seeking health workers of various categories to apply for the opportunity to go and work in Trinidad.

---

[56] Ministry of Health Human Resources for Health Bi-annual Report, July 2014. Ministry of Health, Kampala.
[57] World Health Organization's Global Health Workforce Statistics, OECD, supplemented by country data. https://data.worldbank.org/indicator/SH.MED.PHYS.ZS?locations=UG
[58] World Health Organization. 2008. Establishing and monitoring benchmarks for human resources for health: the workforce density approach. Department of Human Resources for Health, World Health Organization, Geneva. https://www.who.int/hrh/statistics/Spotlight_6_Nov2008_benchmarking.pdf
[59] WHO. Achieving the health-related MDGs. It takes a workforce! https://www.who.int/hrh/workforce_mdgs/en/

> More than 700 health workers applied for the different slots and 283 were shortlisted. Trinidad & Tobago government officials were scheduled to travel to Uganda in December 2014 to conduct the final interviews, to ensure that they got the best of the applicants. While 263 might sound like a small number for a country, the expatriate positions were not being filled from the large pool of unemployed and probably inexperienced health workers, but from those in employment, and in some cases those with teaching responsibilities. The list of those shortlisted included the following: 4 of the country's 11 registered psychiatrists, 20 of Uganda's radiologists, 15 of the 92 pediatricians, 15 of the 126 gynecologists, 15 of the 28 orthopedic (bone and joint) surgeons, 4 of the 15 pathologists, 4 of the 6 urologists, 4 of the 25 ophthalmologists (eye specialists), 15 of Uganda's 91 registered Internal Medicine specialists, and one of the only three neurosurgeons working at the Mulago National Referral hospital. Mulago alone was destined to see 93 of its specialist doctors heading to Trinidad & Tobago. The plans attracted widespread criticism, a lawsuit, and a petition to Parliament initiated by a number of civil society organizations, citing government's failure to protect Ugandans' right to health[60, 61]. Government officials were surprised. They had acted in good faith, they said, to source employment opportunities for 'unemployed' health workers, who would return with superior skills at the end of their two-year contracts.

***

The house might have been a dignified little bungalow back when Mulago Hospital was started, but that would be several decades ago. The place was now dingy without apology. For years it had housed the Skin Clinic, which

---

[60] Sam Okiror. Hospitals in crisis in Uganda as Middle Eastern countries poach medical staff. The Guardian. 25 September 2017. https://www.theguardian.com/global-development/2017/sep/25/hospitals-in-crisis-in-uganda-as-middle-eastern-countries-poach-medical-staff Accessed on 20 June 2019

[61] Elvis Basudde, Juliet Waiswa. Uganda risks losing skilled health workers. New Vision. 22 August 2017

for a short while became important, or rather notorious, because of the many ways in which HIV/AIDS affected the skin. Then more respectable facilities were found, and the Skin Clinic slunk back into the backwaters of a neglected old Mulago.

In 2015 when the Department of Surgery was kicked up the hill from its old home in New Mulago Hospital to make way for the hospital's renovation, the Skin Clinic became its new home. The surgeons must have been under the impression that this was a very temporary address. They did not even bother to put up a decent sign – although to be fair, how does one hang a decent sign on such obvious indecency? The poorly written sign, stuck on the side of some old iron sheets by the wall, was a good match for the structure. Rosemary Nassanga, the head of surgical services and first female urologist in the country, was seated behind a small desk overflowing with papers and files. Across from her office was what looked like a village primary school classroom, complete with rickety wooden chairs. This was now what passed for the surgeons' boardroom. The windows had no glass in them, and the floor was potholed cement, probably from the 1950s. There was no board, and there was no flipchart. There was no white wall on which to project anything. How could anyone think progressive thoughts seated in this place? No wonder the surgeons were staying away from it. Many former occupants of the Surgeons' Boardroom-turned-offices were now baseless.

***

From their inception, Makerere Medical School and Mulago Hospital were made for each other. Or so it seemed. There were spaces for patients and students alike. As long as there had been patients in Mulago, there had been doctors to treat them, and students to learn. Mulago Hospital's role as a teaching hospital was well acknowledged, and the hospital's benefit from the highly skilled and dependable university staff was undisputed. The very early medical research that made Makerere famous, such as work on Burkitt's lymphoma, Kaposi sarcoma, malnutrition, liver cancer, and endomyocardial fibrosis, was done by clinicians who seamlessly rolled their patient care, teaching, and research into one integral job as Mulago doctors. Research funds were lean, and the additional hours a doctor spent on researching their favorite subject were not billed specifically.

But that was then. Not so the new generation of researchers. It appeared that while there might have been many factors that frayed the decades-old harmonious relationship between Mulago and Makerere, the financial rewards of research in the face of much hardship for those engaged purely in patient care was the true fault line. There was a sense that those that got research funding were well paid, and flying off to foreign capitals to talk about their patients, who were in the meantime cared for by their colleagues with no research grants. As might be expected in a complex organization, there were surely many doctors on both sides of the divide who did not fit these descriptions. It would seem that there was enough of a pattern though, that it was only a matter of time before the resentment set in.

The matter seemed to have come to a head under Dr. Edward Ddumba, the hospital's director between 2006 and 2010. He is reported to have said that he did not want to supervise people he did not hire and could not fire – in reference to heads of departments who were Makerere academic faculty. According to some, many academic personnel were too busy doing research to actually look after patients, or even teach. The bigger the grant, it was said, the less likely the Principal Investigator was to teach or care for patients. One head of department had not been to the wards in years, with the occasional exception of participating in the examination of students he had not taught. Ddumba appointed departmental heads employed by Mulago, in effect creating competing heads within every clinical department. The rift between the two institutions was thus formalized.[62]

By 2015 the gentleman's agreement that had been the basis for Makerere and Mulago's comfortable relationship had stopped working. The relationship was neither gentle nor dependent on just men. Dr. Doreen Birabwa-Male,

---

[62] Ddumba believed that there was a need for staff below the deputy director whose primary responsibility was patient care, and he did not see the heads of academic departments fitting this role.

a pediatric surgeon, was now Deputy Director of the hospital, and Prof. Harriet Mayanja had just completed her term as Dean of the School of Medicine. There were many other prominent women in both clinical disciplines and administration.[63] But some in Mulago's leadership were threatening to close its doors on students because they said the resources being availed were for patient care and not education. It was time to put the nature of the relationship in writing.

For the first time in the history of the two institutions, a memorandum of understanding was drawn up to formalize the relationship between Mulago Hospital and the College of Health Sciences. It was signed by the Ministry of Health and Makerere University. That should have settled things. It did not. The framers of the memorandum either overlooked, or avoided inclusion of the one statement that removes ambiguity from all relationships intended to be monogamous: 'to the exclusion of all others'.

The ink was hardly dry on the memorandum when Mulago swung her doors wide open to other suitors. Universities with medical programs and no hospitals were calling. Mulago, with her large pool of patients and a sizable staff was very attractive, and she knew it. Makerere was alarmed. What happened to the relationship? First, it was a threesome, then a square, and more kept coming. There was talk of other memoranda with institutions such as St. Augustine University - which advertised itself as the largest private medical school in the country – Clarke International University, Kibuli Hospital, and Aga Khan University.

The situation was aptly described by Prof. Charles Ibingira, Principal of the College of Health Sciences. "One of the biggest challenges is that despite our MOU, and what we know that Mulago was accredited for Makerere as a teaching hospital, Mulago has gone ahead to welcome other medical schools, bringing their students for training. That would not be a bad idea, but it is not matched by the right number of faculty, and the numbers of patients. There are a number of ethical issues – you find a patient

---

[63] Women who headed departments before 2016 included Prof. Florence Mirembe (Obstetrics & Gynecology), Prof. Sarah Kiguli (Pediatrics), Dr. Agatha Nambuya (Endocrinology, Nuclear Medicine), Dr. Margaret Okello (Anesthesia), Dr. Margaret Mungherera (Psychiatry), Dr. Elsie Kiguli-Malwadde (Radiology).

surrounded by 200 students ... that is the biggest challenge. Most of those schools send the students without any lecturers – so they agree with Mulago that her staff will help them to train their students. What then happens is that they scavenge on Makerere faculty. When our lecturers are teaching, these other students also come in. You cannot send them away, and the universities have a formal arrangement with Mulago. But it is only Makerere whose faculty are now teaching. It would be very difficult, and probably unethical, for staff of those universities to come into Mulago and treat patients in order to teach their students."

There might have been an evolving ethical minefield, but the Mulago Hospital Director was not ambiguous about the hospital's role in training doctors. "Mulago is not a university hospital. It is a teaching hospital, but it is neither owned nor ran by Makerere University's College of Health Sciences. Its growth should not be held back by the College and its training needs. Mulago has chosen its growth path. It is specializing. This is not a good environment in which to teach undergraduates. The undergraduate student needs a general ward where they can see a whole mix of conditions. If the College keeps sending their undergraduates here, some of them will spend their rotations on an infectious diseases ward, and they may never see a patient with a kidney problem. They may never clerk a patient with a heart condition. How are they going to manage these patients once they encounter them in the field?"

Dr. Byarugaba Baterana, known to everyone in Mulago simply as BB, was not one to mince his words. He was slight of build and easy to miss in a crowd, but he more than made up for it by his razor sharp thinking, and his unabashed use of the power of his office. "There are other hospitals – Kiruddu and Kawempe. That is where most of the undergraduate learning should happen, and those hospitals have spaces for teaching. There, they will see general patients, which is what they need. They need to see normal obstetrics. They will see plenty of that there. I think that is why the College of Health Sciences wants to go and build their own hospital, and I would advise them to do just that. Build a university hospital where the general patients can be available to the students. Because here they will only find specializations."[64]

Asked what he planned to do with the graduate students who were a major part of the hospital workforce, and without who Mulago might not function, BB was quick to answer. "Now, the post-graduates – Mulago doors are as open to them as church doors. But there is a problem with the admissions from the College. Mulago will determine how many such students it needs. We want to have an optimum number that we can take on, pay, and hold accountable. The College may admit as many as they want, but they should find some other hospital where they will train them. They would be welcome to attend lectures here, but they must not be on the duty roster, and they must not treat our patients. We do not want people here who we do not pay, and cannot hold accountable."

Makerere's discomfort with student numbers at Mulago was as much a factor of its own growth as the invasion by, or inclusion of, other universities. Ibingira, the College Principal, explained. "Until 1981, the medical school had only one program – the Bachelor of Medicine and Surgery. In 1981 the Bachelor of Dental Surgery (BDS) was introduced, and in 1998 the Bachelors Program in Nursing was added. Without expanding the infrastructure in anyway, other programs have been added. We now have 32 programs – including 13 undergraduate programs. We are adding Masters programs in Emergency Medicine, Neurosurgery, Plastics and Reconstructive Surgery. Most of these students need to access patients. That is why we need more space."

Ibingira and BB were looking at different sides of the exact same coin – patients. If patients were the currency, BB controlled the central bank. "We must have an agreement on who will treat patients. Some members of the faculty only come to do research. They rarely work on patients, and in fact most of them are doing public health research. It is mostly staff of Mulago who are treating patients. The patients are Mulago patients. They

---

[64] Plans were underway for Makerere University College of Health Sciences to build its own 200 bed hospital at Kataremwa, 6.3km north of New Mulago Hospital. Financing mechanisms were being discussed. https://holdings.mak.ac.ug/investorsconference/investment-opportunities/teaching-hospital-at-katalemwa.html

are not Makerere patients. That means I can tell a professor to not come back to the wards, and to not work on patients, and the professor will have to go. It had not happened in the past, but I have done it, and I think it is right. Otherwise we have a lot of doctors who in theory work here, but in practice only very few do, and patients suffer."

Commenting on the strained relationship, Dr. Edward Ddumba recalled from his Mulago days the difficulties of balancing the sometimes conflicting needs of training and patient care. His conclusion was rather philosophical: "The memorandum of understanding – a piece of paper on which people sign – may not solve a problem, unless people have first worked on the relationship. They must understand the genesis of the disharmony. It is not the marriage certificate that creates the marriage."

Patients and their attendants wait outside a ward in New Mulago Hospital, 2012. *Monitor Publications Limited.*

Olive Kobusingye

Patients' relatives wait outside the Maternity Ward at Kabale Regional Referral Hospital, Kabale, Western Uganda. 2014. *Monitor Publications Limited.*

Patients wait at the Outpatient Department of Wol Health Center III in Agago, Northern Uganda. 2012. *Monitor Publications Limited.*

***

Francis and Ntege were having lunch at the students' canteen, wedged between Albert Cook Library on the upper side and Davies Lecture Theatre on the lower side. The place was very busy with both students and teachers, and the seating was limited. The canteen infrastructure had not changed one bit since their student days. Back then, there were just snacks, and only the well-off students could afford them. Most students simply hang around and played chess, or had tea, which was all they could afford. Now there were more elaborate meals, and it seemed like many students could afford them. Outside the canteen were huge campaign posters of the aspirants to the various University Guild and Medical Students' Association positions. In their time, Francis and Ntege could recall that the medical students had not engaged with campus politics. The students' association campaigns were a very modest affair in those days.

"From admitting 120 students a year we have suddenly jumped to three hundred.[65] No extra space, no new arrangements for teaching. So now this is truly telemedicine. Most students do not hear what is going on by the bedside, never mind seeing the patient," Francis said in his now habitually resigned voice. "Today we had a class of more than thirty students in tow on a teaching round. And that's without counting the intern pharmacists, nurses, and whatever other cadre of health worker thinks they can learn something from this largely ceremonial exercise. The greatest asset for a medical student now is a good imagination. They imagine what the patient looks like, what is wrong with them, what the teacher is saying – a pity they are not allowed to imagine stuff for the exams. But the good old clinical exams are gone too. Not enough time, not enough space, not enough patients for students to examine. But there is surely time enough for all that when the students graduate and become interns. So God help the patients!" The two men were quiet for a while.

"Do you know the definition of a failed state?" Francis resumed.

"No. But I am sure we are living in one. I gather yesterday the President was seen carrying a sack of cash, distributing it to village women in western Uganda. At seventy three, or eighty three, or whatever his real age is, moving from one fake SACCO[66] to the next, handing out cash. After thirty years in power, this is his idea of eradicating poverty. Although, truth be told, the President has no interest in eradicating poverty. Poor people are much easier to manipulate.'

"It sounds like those women have said goodbye to poverty for now," chipped in Winnie, who had just joined the two surgeons uninvited.

"These women have no access to health care. Any of them is a candidate for a maternal death should they go into labor and fail to

---

[65] In 2017 the College of Health Sciences admitted a total of 300 first year students for Medicine, Nursing, and Pharmacy. The numbers of students on the wards are further swelled by programs such as Radiography and Palliative Care, as well as other universities which have medical training programs but no teaching hospitals.
[66] Savings and Credit Cooperative Organization

deliver in the banana plantation, as is their practice. If their babies survive infancy, they are likely to get malnutrition, or to die from a preventable infectious disease. The survivors will be found seated under a mango tree, or in a dilapidated shelter that passes for a classroom under the failed Universal Primary Education. So – no, I do not know the definition of a failed state but I know the state of failure when I see it. And I can tell you that this is it."

"You know, it is very difficult for a state to fail. There are too many interests. It is kept alive, somehow." Winnie cut the chicken breast into tiny pieces and mixed them with rice before rolling them into the *chapatti*.

"Which is why, I suppose, they are called failed states, and not dead states. When a business fails the owners close the door and sell the remaining assets. Countries are messier."

There was silence as all three surgeons went back to their food. After a short while Francis started up again.

"Every sector has its rot. There is failure in every sector in this country. But nowhere is it personalized the way it is in health. Children are not learning. They drop out of school barely literate. They become mediocre youths that are unemployed and unemployable. Nobody writes a school failure certificate. These people sooner than later die of something their better educated counterparts managed to avoid. But where do they go to die? In the hands of a health worker. Some unfortunate doctor signs their name on a death certificate. The economy is full of holes. Businesses are defaulting on loans and folding up. Does a government planner sign a death certificate when a business dies? No. But when it dies, the owner and their family are in crisis. No housing, no education, no food. They leave the city and go back to the village. A halfhearted infection walking through the village latches onto them and they come into the hospital to die. A doctor writes the death certificate. In reality, such patients are victims of a dying economy and not the infection. Yet all these deaths are blamed on the doctors who are not managing to prevent them. We can only do so much. We are not miracle workers."

The doctors had had these conversations so many times; it was amazing that they were still in the profession.

President Yoweri Museveni handing an envelope to a farmer in Kamuli during his 'Prosperity for All' tour of Busoga region, 2007. *Monitor Publications Limited*

> Mental freedom cannot exist apart from that of the body. Free thinkers want to become free people too. Rudolf Karl Ludwig Virchow, nineteenth-century German physician (1821-1902).

***

Okello glanced at his cellphone. Ten minutes to 1.00am. He was now resigned to spending all night in the operating room. He had just finished one emergency C-section. There were three others on the ward, all hoping to be done in the next few hours at the latest. A 23 year-old woman that had delivered by C-section twice before was in labor. Ordinarily she should not have been allowed to go into labor, but should have been scheduled for a C-section as soon as the baby was fully grown and ready for delivery. She had spent a week at a health center waiting for the surgery, and had gone into labor while waiting. She was then transferred to Mulago for lack of anesthesia at the health center. The second patient had developed severe eclampsia, a condition in which a pregnant mother develops uncontrollable high blood pressure that threatens both the mother and her unborn baby. Left untreated, the mother usually begins to convulse and often slips into a coma from which she may not recover. She should have been receiving intensive care, but the best the ward could do was to move her into a room close to the nurses' station where they could look in on her more frequently. Even then, there was really no special attention paid to her. The two nurses on duty were too busy to monitor her continuously as required. Her only hope was to get to theater right away and have the baby taken out, hopefully still alive. The third emergency was a teenager with a narrow pelvis that had made little progress since her labor started several hours before. She was still stable, and would have to wait. But the real problem now was that there was no theatre linen. Okello and his team had no sterile linen to use for the operations. The OR was supplied with enough linen for four operations at the beginning of the day, and they were now exhausted. They would have to wait for the linen to be washed and sterilized. Given the hour, it was unlikely that there was anyone in the laundry department worrying about Okello and his emergencies. He was still thinking through his options when the OR door swung open. "Dr. Okello, which patient is coming next? You had indicated the patient with two previous scars but the eclampsia really can't wait. We have failed to control the convulsions. The fetal heart is erratic ...,"

"Neither patient is coming," Okello cut her short. "No linen."

"What?! If we lose another patient this week there will be hell to pay. I am sending the eclampsia patient." The Sister-in-Charge of Maternity stood in the door for a short while, then walked out, leaving the doors to swing closed. "What am I supposed to do?", Okello shouted at her receding frame. "I do not control the Laundry." It was the third night this week that operations would not be completed for lack of supplies. The first time he was not on call, but he had heard that the OR had run out of oxygen. The second time there had been no linen, and by the time the linen arrived the anesthetist had left. On both nights there were maternal deaths.

"Bring the eclampsia patient," Okello called to the theatre attendant who sat dozing in the corner. Then under his breath, "We shall have to operate her without the linen. Better to battle the inevitable infection than wait for the equally inevitable result if we do not operate." Having made that decision, he was suddenly energized. He went to find the anesthetist who was playing games on his cellphone in recovery room. "The next patient is on her way. Eclampsia." The anesthetist, Mr. Balinda, looked up. "You got the linen?"

"No. I got a threat from the Sister-in-Charge. We shall just have to work with no linen. I hope we have enough mops." Balinda shrugged and got up. His job was to put the patient to sleep. Let the doctor worry about the linen. At least tonight he had enough oxygen. He had reviewed the eclampsia patient at the beginning of the shift when he saw the theatre list, and was relieved that they were going to start with her.

***

> Turning and turning in the widening gyre
> The falcon cannot hear the falconer;
> Things fall apart; the center cannot hold;
> Mere anarchy is loosed upon the world,
> The blood-dimmed tide is loosed, and everywhere
> The ceremony of innocence is drowned;
> The best lack all conviction, while the worst
> Are full of passionate intensity.

The second coming, William Butler Yeats, 1865 - 1939

***

"Which of you is willing to remain at work while the rest of us go on strike?"

"There is a strike?" Okello was just coming in from the ward.

"Which hole are you crawling out of? We have had it coming for more than a week. But it has now been formally declared. Begins tomorrow at 9.00am. Only skeleton staff to work on emergencies. Of course that means that we work pretty much as usual, given that we have been doing only emergencies for a long while anyway. When was the last time any of you scheduled and actually worked on non-emergency cases?" Mugisha was usually the best informed of the Obs/Gyn PG room occupants. He had both feet firmly plugged into student politics, and though he was a dedicated student who rarely left the hospital, he could be relied upon to know what was going on beyond the hospital walls.

***

The struggle by Ugandan health workers for better pay was as old as the health service. The first Ugandan (indigenous) health workers to be employed in the government health system were initially trained as dressers and assistants. When the training of clinicians started, the titles and positions remained contentious for decades. In the forties, the highest position a Ugandan could aspire to was that of African Assistant Medical Officer (AAMO), which was itself an improvement from the much detested African Native Medical Assistant. These health workers constantly agitated for better pay. In 1946 the salary of an AAMO increased from £156 to £315 per annum. In 2018 terms the officer would have earned £1,079 per month. The insult of poor pay was made worse by the glaring inequality between the races – the Ugandan medical officer's salary was half that of the white European Nursing Sister. At that time indigenous Ugandans were by law barred from engaging in private practice even after retirement. When this legal barrier was removed in 1949, there was rapid attrition, with doctors leaving poorly paying government jobs to set up their own private practices. The government responded by increasing salaries to try and keep doctors in government employment. In 1951 a medical officer earned the equivalent of £1,059 a year (equivalent to £28,216, or US$22,179.00 in 2019). In 1953 it was raised to £1,237, and further to £1,982 in 1954. By 1955 the annual take home was £2,873, equivalent to £56,453 in 2018. Salaries were not the only source of unhappiness. Doctors especially complained about poor housing, inadequate equipment in hospitals, inadequate professional support especially in upcountry stations, and a lack of recognition and status by the colonial administration. In subsequent decades the salaries stabilized, until the seventies when all civil service salaries started to go down. At that time the Director General of Health Services was the highest paid officer in the entire civil service, and senior medical consultants were at the same salary scale as high court judges.

Medical workers started to agitate for better pay, and over the years they threatened, and very occasionally staged short lived strikes that did not result in better pay or improved conditions. In 1995 a nationwide sit-down-strike organized by the Uganda Medical Workers Union paralyzed health facilities for a few days. The Union's leaders were arrested and imprisoned, and when they were released they stayed on Police Bond reporting monthly for more than a year. Salaries were only marginally raised after that strike. By 2004 junior doctors earned a basic salary of US$250 (UGX506,000) per month. Enrolled nurses earned $100 (UGX210,000) while clinical officers earned US$160 (UGX350,000). Health workers' demands that a doctor earn at least US$400 (UGX800,000), clinical officers US$350 (UGX700,000), and enrolled nurses US$160 (UGX350,000) were outright rejected, and the health workers were threatened with dismissal. Between 2012 and 2018 there were at least 20 documented strikes by health workers, the most widespread being in 2017. Despite the Uganda Medical Association leadership having followed all the professional procedures required of medical workers planning industrial action, the Minister of Health declared the strike illegal, and the President threatened the doctors with arrest, mass dismissals, and replacement with recruits from Cuba.

To make his point, eight (8) military doctors were deployed to replace the hundreds of striking doctors at Mulago Hospital. A Ministry of Health delegation visited Cuba to explore the prospects of recruiting Cuban doctors to either augment or replace Ugandan ones. **Sources**: John Eliffe, *East African Doctors*, Cambridge University Press, 1998, New York. Alexander Odonga, *Makerere Medical School 1924 – 1974*, Marianum Press, Kisubi, Uganda. Edward K. Kanyesigye. Opinion: Selective salary reward for health workers: realistic or a distortion? *Health Policy and Development*; 1 (1): 3-5 UMU Press 2003

***

Francis was just leaving the hospital when he got a call from a former schoolmate. "Francis, are you at the hospital?"

"No," he lied. "Why?"

"My nephew is admitted on Orthopedic Ward. He has been there for three weeks waiting for an emergency operation." Despite his fatigue and the anxiety in his friend's voice Francis burst out laughing.

"If he has waited for three weeks it was clearly not an emergency."

"Well, that is what the doctors said." Francis was only half listening as the friend launched into a detailed explanation of the injury that left the young man lying in the orthopedic ward. The friend only hung up after Francis promised to check on him the following day. As soon as he got off the phone he realized he had left his car a short distance away from the ward where the young man was. He might as well get this done and over with, he thought.

Francis walked past the Rodney Belcher Department of Orthopedics building, round the back to the former Psychiatry wards that now served as the orthopedic trauma wards. The big sign for 'Bbosa Mental Health Ward' was still in place at the entrance to the outpatient clinic that now housed the orthopedic clinic. It was named after the late Prof. Bbosa, the first Ugandan psychiatrist. Three beds were lined up in the open along the walkway, and their occupants looked like they were fresh admissions, evidence that there was no more space inside the ward. Francis walked past the beds into the ward, and made his way down the narrow space between patients' beds to get to the nurses' station. At a few minutes to five in the evening, he knew there was little chance of finding any staff on duty, but he was in luck. He spotted a white coat bent over a bed farther down and made a beeline for it. A clinical officer he knew well was completing a plaster cast on a child's leg.

"Yes Musumba, how are you doing?"

"Fine, just leaving…"

"I am looking for a young man that is waiting for theatre. Bosco Kiganda"

"Oh yes. He is over there," he said, pointing to the far corner. "He has a fracture right femur and left tibia fibula. He has been waiting for money for the implant. The mother says they are getting it tomorrow." The two men moved closer to the young man in the corner.

"For three weeks? With no traction?" Francis could see there was only a flimsy looking string held in place by a crepe bandage, the string itself held taut by a small jerrycan dangling at the foot of the bed. This was somebody's idea of traction, clearly grossly inadequate. Francis did not need to look at the X-rays. The middle of the thigh looked like a balloon, and the leg was lying with the foot pointing outwards, a sign that there was no alignment at the fracture site. The crepe bandage and string were purely cosmetic, serving no traction purpose.

"Yes," Musumba responded. "We have no equipment to put up proper traction. When we moved from New Mulago all the traction beams were discarded, and we were told that these fractures would be operated on an emergency basis. The traction was said to be old fashioned. But now the patients are required to buy the implants, and those that do not have the money have no option but wait like this. Occasionally we get donations of implants from visiting surgeons, but they don't last very long. That is why this ward is so crowded. We cannot operate on the patients, and we cannot discharge them."

Francis looked around him. There were patients of all ages, in all manner of postures and positions. Some had plaster casts on their limbs. Some casts were visibly filthy, with dried up blood marking the sites of the wounds underneath. An open wound here, bloody gauze dressings there. A catheter running into a urine bag on the floor, empty bottles hanging on nails by the window. Hardly any space between patients, every patient with their choice of beddings in every imaginable sanitary state. Two patients lay on the floor in the corner, and save for the plastic sheeting covering the thin mattresses, they had no bedding. One could smell the toilets from the ward entrance. The chaos on the wards had become so routine that for orthopedic patients hoping for a sterile operation this was asking for a miracle. The bacteria in these wards were spoilt for choice. How many patients came here with simple fractures and intact skin, and went home with deadly infections in their bones?

"You should talk to Mr. Sekimpi, sir. He has a theater list on Thursday. Maybe if the patient has found money for the implant by then, he can be on the list. Otherwise he will have to wait till after the Easter holidays," Musumba said.

Francis thanked the Clinical Officer and left the ward. He would tell his friend to forget about Mulago. This was not a hospital where people came to get better. Those that did get better would probably have gotten better in their homes. And truth be told, some patients were worse off for coming to Mulago, where there was the illusion that some care was being given. Only the desperate were coming here. Francis had never actively participated in any industrial action, but he thought the plans for industrial action beginning the following day might be a good idea. The young man waiting for operation for three weeks would have to wait longer, but maybe future patients might get better services if the strike was successful. As he walked towards the car, he was struck by the irony. The old was discarded as backward and inefficient. The new was out of reach because of the cost. People like Kiganda fell through the wide void between the old and the new. The leap between the one and the other was fraught with many dangers. There in the crevasses lay misplaced faith, greed, and ignorance.

Francis got into his car and headed for the Surgeons' Parade in Kololo, where he often made more from doing one operation than he earned for a whole month of working in Mulago.

***

The Patient

> 'It is the curse of humanity that it learns to tolerate even the most horrible situations by habituation. ... education, wealth and freedom are the only guarantee for the permanent health of a population.'
> Rudolf Karl Ludwig Virchow, nineteenth-century German physician (1821-1902).

By 2019, the New Mulago renovations were going into their fifth year. The iron sheets that had blocked the construction from view were aging. All the work had been expected to take less than two years. Periodically, a new date for reopening was named, and each one passed without any sign of completion. Medical students that had previously needed only a few minutes to move between wards and the library, or the morgue, or the lecture theatres depending on the program for the day, were now faced with the monumental task of moving between campuses several kilometers apart between sessions. Kampala's notorious traffic jams only made things worse. Lecturers that had effortlessly combined teaching and patient care on one location now had to plan more carefully, in order to manage the burdensome commutes.

Very close to the Mulago Hill summit more construction was taking place. The four-storied structure housing the Uganda Cancer Institute shielded the construction from casual observers. This was phenomenal growth from the institute's humble beginnings in the ancient looking bungalows farther down the hill. In 2008, the Institute had formalized collaboration with the Seattle-based Fred Hutch Cancer Center, a partnership that set the stage for phenomenal growth in the capacity for cancer research and care. The modern three-level UCI - Fred Hutch Cancer Center sat a few feet away from the old bungalows, and contained state-of-the-art labs, offices, and clinics where patients got care that had previously not been available in the country.

Dr. Henry Ddungu, one of the Institute's specialist doctors, was exuberant. "In the next few years the situation of cancer care will change. We are putting up a radiotherapy center – it will perhaps be the biggest of its kind in Sub-Saharan Africa. The building will accommodate four linear accelerators[67], in addition to the Cobalt-60 machine we have now. We are expanding all the

---

[67] Modern radiotherapy equipment

services. We are putting another five levels on this building." It was hard not to share Ddungu's enthusiasm, with the construction crew in full view outside his office window on Level 4. He pointed to the construction site. "There is another building – a multipurpose structure. It will have surgical suites, bone marrow transplant suites, lecture rooms, offices ... there will be a whole floor for childhood cancer treatment. We are changing the face of cancer care in the region. Within country we are opening up regional centers – Mbarara is already open. Arua and Mbale are coming up. Once the funding becomes available, these regional centers will be active. The Kyadondo Cancer Registry is still running, and we are beginning a registry in Gulu." [68]

Indeed, things were looking up for the Institute. The East African Community had designated it a Center of Excellence in Cancer care for the region.

A 2016 Act of Parliament had freed the Cancer Institute from its historical ties to Mulago – and by implication, from relying on the National Medical Stores for its supplies. "That was a very big victory for us," Ddungu affirmed. "We had suffered under the NMS – stock-outs, very expensive purchases, we were not in control of our own budgets. Many issues were not clear. Right now we have more than 70% of the medicines we need. We have been able to buy quality products at very reasonable prices. We are making big savings. Cutting out the middleman was great."

To say that 'many issues were not clear' was perfect Ugandan-speak. There had in fact been bitter battles fought between the Cancer Institute and the National Medical Stores over money and control. It was hard to imagine a more vulnerable population than the patients that huddled around the Cancer Institute's over-crowded wards, many from distant districts, with no relations in Kampala, and therefore entirely dependent on Mulago for sustenance during the long treatment stays. Often, the family camped on one of the verandas, and the patient could count on at most one free meal a day. The rest, the family had to find, somehow. They did all they had to do, to be sure that the patient stayed alive to receive the precious anti-cancer

---

[68] The Kampala Cancer Registry is the oldest continuously kept such registry in Africa. It registered its first cases in 1951, and through all the turmoil, the registry was kept running by little-known custodians, pathologists who at times personally visited various hospitals to keep their records updated.

treatment depending on the treatment regimen. But with the NMS versus Cancer Institute wars raging, very often the medicines were out of stock. There might be weeks, or even months of waiting, of missed doses, of hopes raised and hopes dashed. Doctors that first admitted patients when they believed they had a fighting chance to rid the patients of the cancer saw those chances whittled away by lack of the right medicines. The doctors and nurses had to put on brave faces, and to continue to reassure the patients that they were doing all they could to help them. Those with some means would ask for prescriptions in order to buy the medicines from private pharmacies. Anti-cancer medicines were not cheap though, and only a small minority could afford them. Dr. Jackson Orem, the Institute's soft spoken director, had stood before every conceivable committee from the hospital through to the Ministry of Health and Parliament, to plead the case for cancer patients. The autonomy had been well argued and hard earned.

In 2006, the Uganda government supported the establishment of a local pharmaceutical manufacturing company, Quality Chemicals Limited, to promote local pharmaceutical production. Government was so persuaded about its business case that it signed a memorandum of understanding that bound the government (through National Medical Stores) to buy all its Anti-Retroviral drugs (ARVs) from the company - a monopoly, to make sure that it got a foot on the growth ladder before being subjected to open competition. With production happening at home, and with the guaranteed market, the prices should have been low. Not so. A value-for-money audit done in 2016[69] revealed that in fact in the majority of cases, the prices at which National Medical Stores (NMS) procured ARVs from Quality Chemicals Limited during the period under review were higher than the prices of drugs imported under donor supported arrangements. The differences in pricing were substantial, and on average more than 25%. Equally disturbing, the country's dependence on donors for the provision of ARVs had increased over the years, instead of going down. The percentage of quantities of ARVs donated had grown from 58% to 80% of the total ARV supplies in 2015. Something was not right. But the disadvantageous price differentials were not limited to ARVs. One of the main explanations for the perennial stock-outs of anti-cancer medicines was that NMS was pricing the medicines it sourced far higher than comparable international (WHO median) prices. The mark-up was in many cases higher than 200% of the international prices. In the two most extreme cases, the NMS prices of commonly used medicines were 1,795% and 2,590% higher than WHO international median prices. It was hard to see how the NMS could possibly be working in the interests of Ugandan patients. An autonomous Uganda Cancer Institute was managing to get its medicines at far cheaper rates, and to avoid disruptive stock-outs.

---

[69] Annual Report of The Auditor General for the Audit Year ended December 2016. Volume 5. Value for money Audit. Office of the Auditor General. Kampala, Uganda. 2016

"The Institute has that history - the culture of cancer research that is unmatched in the region. That is partly why it was chosen as a center of excellence for the region." Dr. Jackson Orem, Director, Uganda Cancer Institute.

***

The rumors that had swirled around Makerere University regarding cheating and other malpractices in student assessment remained largely unsubstantiated. People talked of 'sex for marks' deals. There was said to be a racket in some university departments involving the sale of exam papers, the alteration of marks if a student had failed a paper but had enough money, or if they were willing to exchange sexual favors for a better mark than they got in the exams.

A member of faculty at the College of Health Sciences who had tried to fight the vice said cheating was rampant. "Students used to come to the medical school from all corners of the country. Now only a handful of well-known urban schools are bringing students to the medical school. Moreover, once they get here, some are assisted to pass. There is a lot of wasted potential out there in the countryside. Beware which doctor you go to see. Some should never have been allowed into the school, let alone to graduate with the Hippocratic oath." Many people would have thought the lecturer was being extreme. Occasionally a whistle blower cried foul, but proof of the mischief was elusive. In October 2018 that was to change.

With little warning on a hill that carried seven rumors a day, the bombshell dropped. Makerere University fired two members of staff and demoted two others over what they called gross misconduct, related to falsifying students' marks, and smuggling names of failed students onto the graduating roll. The sacked employees were not junior clerks altering students' exam scripts. The deputy academic registrar of the College of Health Sciences, Fatuma Nakatudde, and Senior Administrative Assistant Paul Apunyo, had allegedly managed to hack into the computerized examinations system and changed the marks of at least two students. They then got the students' names onto the graduation roll. In the fallout, fifty-nine other students whose presence on the graduation roll was suspect were taken off the list, and some 14,000 academic transcripts were held back. The School of Medicine was not implicated, but troubles in the School of Health Sciences were too close for comfort. Across the institution, there was a sigh of relief. It appeared that sanity was at last being restored. The Ivory Tower's gleam might have been smudged, but the cleanup was underway. At least that is what everyone hoped.

***

The long and tiring trip that had started at 5.00am in Kanungu was coming to an end. The bus was making its way down Namirembe Road on the southern end of the city, heading for the bus park in the heart of Kampala. The vehicle traffic was fairly light, but progress was slow because of the heavy pedestrian traffic. Vendors were literally hugging the bus, shoving their merchandise at the passengers. Chewing gum, fake jewelry, shoes, children's books, the Kabaka's portrait pictures. Muscular men were weaving through traffic with wheelbarrows full of pineapples and *matoke*, undeterred by the incessant honking. For many village folk who were unfamiliar with Kampala this was all new and exciting, perhaps even bewildering. For Kweete this was very familiar. She had made this trip at least three times a year for her review at Mulago hospital's medical outpatient clinic. Most times she returned on the assigned day, but this time she was coming a couple of weeks early because she was feeling unusually tired. She had a cough that she failed to shake off for close to a month. Sitting on a bus for 10 hours had not helped, and by the time she got off, she was beginning to feel faint. She had planned to cross South Street into the Old Taxi Park where she would get a taxi to Bukoto, but as she stepped off the pavement into South Street, she was suddenly engulfed by a wave of dizziness. She felt the bottom of her stomach contract violently, and she started retching. She seemed to be floating rather than walking. As reality merged with illusion, all she could see was a sea of rainbows. The ground was rushing up to meet her face. Why were so many cars honking?

Were those screeching brakes? Was that her bag flying away, high above the rainbows?

***

A physician examined Kweete and determined that she had an acute endomyocarditis – an inflammation of the heart muscle and its inner lining. The heart muscle was too weak to pump the blood from its chambers, first into the lungs to pick up oxygen, and then into the rest of the body to deliver the oxygen. With the valves flip-flopping and the muscles working only halfheartedly, the chambers started to flood and the body became starved of oxygen. Clearly, Kweete's heart problems had not started on the bus. Her heart had been failing slowly over time, and it had finally exhausted its reserve capacity.

***

The eastern face of Mulago Hill were slowly taking on a new look. The years of construction seemed to be coming to a close, at least on the exterior. An imposing new gate that towered several meters in the air announced Mulago National Specialized Hospital. For the moment though, the gate remained closed. Traffic from Kira and Upper Mulago Hill roads was still using a narrow and badly potholed side entrance that brought one within a few meters of the School of Public Health. Outside the gate, and for most of the short distance between Kira Rd and the new gate, fruit vendors displayed their offers, some on plastic sheets, others on wheelbarrows, many on the bare ground. The pavement was their space, and pedestrians had to pick their way carefully in order to avoid upsetting the little mounds of mangoes, oranges, and passion fruit. A *boda-boda* stage at the entrance to the Nurses' Hostel took up most of the pavement to the right and extended into the road, further narrowing the space.

Inside the gate and away from the chaos outside, the transformation of the 57 year-old New Mulago Hospital into a modern super-specialized wonder was in the final stages. Dr. Henry Mwebesa, the acting Director General of Health Services at the Ministry of Health, and the man in charge of the multi-million dollar Mulago project, could not say enough glorious things about the facility. "If you go to the ICU, the equipment you will find was the latest on the market in 2018 – even St. Thomas Hospital in London does not have it. Then in the 22 operating theaters, you will find cameras and screens for display, so students will not have to be in the room to see what is going on – new design lights, there are no oxygen cylinders, all the oxygen is piped … so what you will find here is what you will find in the most modern hospitals in Dubai, in Europe, in the US – in fact it is exactly what you will find in one of Texas' best – the Texas Pediatric Hospital, which is also new." It all sounded wonderful, until one thought of the difference between Uganda's and Texas' budgets, and what it must cost the Texas Pediatric Hospital to maintain its cutting-edge equipment, and the people that use and take care of it. How likely was it that an operating room assistant or nurse in Texas might steal detergent or batteries to sell them, lest their children go to bed hungry?

A little farther up the Upper Mulago Hill Road to the right, a brand new four-story building stood in the space between the decades-old Galloway medical students' hostel and the Queen Elizabeth Nurses' Hostel – the new Women and Neonatal Hospital. It was such a source of pride that it was formally opened twice – first by Prime Minister Ruhakana Rugunda, and in case a few obstinate doors had remained closed, by the President a few weeks later. The opening was received with excitement and skepticism in equal measure. Some feared that it would be unaffordable. With its spacious rooms and corridors, a well fitted newborn ICU and suites, and elevators that actually worked, those patients that could afford it were surely going to receive a fine service.

For a country with a serious shortage of well-equipped medical facilities, which this was, the hospital was curiously empty. The parking lot was almost bare, and a stroll into the main lobby – once one got past the metal detectors at the entrance – was equally quiet. At its opening, the Minister of Health was categorical – this was a referral hospital, for complex conditions that could not be treated at lower levels. But the important distinction between the patients being treated here and those seen in upper Mulago would not be how ill they were, or that the illnesses had baffled doctors at lower level facilities. Important as these were, the determining factor would be the ability to pay. Without health insurance, and without being 'entitled', one would have to pay upfront. A C-section here cost the equivalent of a registered nurse's earnings for two months, before medicines and other hospital charges.

In reality the gate between the old and the new, between Upper Mulago and the lower super-specialized facility was guarded by a cashier and not by a fence or a security guard. So right here, in the heart of Kampala, were the neocolonial versions of Entebbe Grade A and Entebbe Grade B. The hospital was built using public funds, the government having borrowed US$49 million from the Islamic Development Bank. The health workers, drawn from the existing Mulago workforce, were paid directly from the public purse. The majority of people who would be paying back the loans through their taxes could not afford to use the services of the hospital.

New Mulago Hospital, showing levels 3 (Accident & Emergency Department under the bridge), and 4 – 6, front block. 2006. *Monitor Publications Limited*

Main entrance to Mulago National Specialised Hospital, September 2019, still closed for renovation. *Monitor Publications Limited*

There was a sharp distinction between the old and the new. Old Mulago had old and dilapidated buildings, unavailable or dysfunctional medical equipment, and poorly motivated medical workers. But that would be too simplistic for a complex organization like Mulago, itself a microcosm of the whole country. Amidst the dysfunction one could find pockets of order and efficiency. The former ICU now housed a cancer treatment unit, and doctors here were world class experts. It was a puzzle why they were not part of the Uganda Cancer Institute – one of many puzzles on this hill, where international collaborations and foreign money often caused distortions in the structures. The massive Baylor Uganda, 'a clinical Center of Excellence on the campus of Mulago Hospital', in essence a hospital within a hospital – was providing HIV/AIDS care and treatment to HIV-infected children and family members. Patients here did not seem to belong to BB's economy.

***

In 2010 the Ministry of Health had embarked on plans to build two new hospitals in Kampala in order to decongest Mulago, and allow it to carry out its true mandate of being a national referral and teaching hospital. In addition, Mulago would be renovated and upgraded. Works at Mulago were to include a specialized hospital for women and newborn babies. The scope of work was estimated at US$51 million, and equipment another USD 22 million. (The women's hospital was estimated to cost US$33 million. Kiruddu and Kawempe hospitals were each estimated at US$4 (four) million. A couple of millions more would be spent on training, purchase of computer software, and such other expenses.) The Ministry turned to the African Development Bank (AfDB) for funding. After a series of negotiations, AfDB approved a concessional loan of US$23.4 million for the New Mulago upgrade, and facilitated the negotiations to have the Islamic Development Bank finance the Women and Newborn hospital through another concessional loan. The New Mulago design work was complete in 2012, and in 2013 the tendering process began. ROKO Construction Limited had the best bid, and at USD25 million, it compared very favorably with the USD23.4 million that had been budgeted and secured from AfDB. As soon as the first hammer hit the concrete, the ghosts struck back – the mortuary wall, where another level was supposed to be added, crumbled. The structure's integrity was found wanting in some places. In the meantime, Ministry of Health officials were traveling the globe to 'bench-mark' with other hospitals. It started to appear unwise to do only modest renovations, which might require that more work be done after only a few years, when the opportunity was here to do all of what was necessary to transform the old hospital into a modern one. Once that thinking took center stage, the designs started to change – quite radically. The original design had an inferior floor – that was changed to linoleum flooring and walls. The old windows which were to be preserved to cut costs were literally thrown out of the windows, and aluminum sliding windows were installed, allowing the inclusion of a mesh to keep out mosquitoes. The old flush doors – were flushed out. The contractor would not hear of so much new wine being poured into old bottles. The serious upgrade was not in the windows and floors, though. The operating capacity was increased several-fold to give 22 operating rooms, the Intensive Care Unit was greatly expanded, and a whole kidney transplant unit that had not existed in the original design was created. All these changes raised the cost by an extra US$14 million. The whole project had been envisaged to take two years. Four years later the AfDB money ran out and the work was nowhere near finished. Some of the equipment which had been ordered anticipating timely completion arrived, and started to gather dust – literally, in addition to running out of the warranty period. The Ministry of Health ran to Ministry of Finance and explained that US$14 million was needed to finish the work. After some considerable haggling, US$6 million was released. The contractor was only partially appeased. Work could resume, but only just. As the injection started to run out, so did the pace of work. The media and the public soon picked up the story that work had stalled. This could not have happened at a worse time – Ministry of Finance was on one hand saying it did not have the US$8 million to complete Mulago, but it had just managed to find US$397 million to loan to a foreign investor who was planning to build another hospital - a private hospital it seemed – whose foundation stone had not even been laid.[70] The Mulago medical community was aghast. Specialist surgeons who had spent the preceding two years getting additional training in order to use the upgraded facilities such as the kidney transplant unit were devastated. A leading heart surgeon left the country in disgust, and was quickly snapped up by a hospital in Botswana. It took public protests, petitions from doctors' associations, parliamentary debates and lobbying, to persuade Finance that providing the USD8 million might after all be the right thing to do.

***

---

[70] The Secretary to the Treasury, Keith Muhakanizi, explained that this money was not a loan, but rather promissory notes to the investor, FINASI from Italy, and that once the hospital was completed and running, the government of Uganda would pay over a period of six years.

"The government has done a major catch-up job. To dig the country out of the decades-old shortage of hospital beds, they have renovated the old 1,200-bed facility, and now it has an astounding 350 beds!" Nambasi, a Senior House Officer in Surgery, was making the commentary in PG room as he and other colleagues waited to start a tutorial on the operative management of complicated femoral fractures.

"What? You are shameless." Karegyeya and Nambasi rarely agreed on anything. "You may not like the government, and God knows it has earned some of the bad press that it gets, but you need to give credit where it is due. The 350 beds are only for the super-specialized hospital. You should count the 400 beds in the brand new Women and Newborn Hospital, the 170 beds at Kawempe, and the 200 beds at Kiruddu."

Nambasi was quick to retort. "Well, if you do the math you will realize that all those put together still come short of the original 1200 beds before the renovation. But if it makes you feel better, we are now back where we were 50 years ago. Most planners look ahead to project the services that will be needed by future populations. I should give credit to our hind-sighted leaders who are one better. Why rush ahead? In the next financial year, they might propel us forward. We have been marking time for the last 50 years."

"If you are referring to the projections made in the 1950s, remember that many of the health centers and private hospitals that now exist in the greater Kampala area did not exist then. So we should plan within the current context, and not use the historical context as you seem to suggest."

"You do not tire of defending the indefensible." Nambasi was now fired up. "Decent private facilities are inaccessible to the majority of the people who need health care. Some who go to those facilities can barely afford two meals a day. They are desperate. Patients are selling family assets to afford a night in a private hospital. The system is set up to milk the poor in order to make it possible for the wealthy to get privileged services."

***

In December 2011 a financial performance report prepared for the Office of the Prime Minister revealed that the government was spending at least US$150 million (about Shs400b in 2011) on treatment of top government officials abroad annually.[71] This did not include non-medical costs such as air tickets, accompanying family or attendants' lodging and upkeep. The revelation sparked criticism from various circles, and the President instructed that the responsible ministries look into ways to bring the costs down. The Ministry of Health responded by disputing the report's estimates, and instead said that the annual costs were about US$2.2m (Shs5.8b).[72] (In 2019 when government needed to justify the approval of public funds for a private investor to construct a hospital, they revised this figure to US$123 million for 2016, for only India bound patients.) Civil society organizations protested the insensitive hemorrhage of public resources, and argued that the money would be better spent in upgrading the medical facilities at home. In July 2017, following the death of a former government minister at a private clinic in Kampala, the Speaker of Parliament Honorable Rebecca Kadaga called for faster tracking of approvals for government officers wishing to go abroad for treatment. She described the existing due process as frustrating.[73] The former minister had died of advanced cancer, and had in fact sought care abroad early

---

[71] Ismail Musa Ladu. Government spends Shs380 billion on officials' treatment abroad. The Monitor. 24 April 2012

[72] Ismail Musa Ladu. Shs204b spent abroad because Uganda cannot treat her own. The Monitor. 5 November 2014

[73] Nelson Wesonga. Ease travel for treatment abroad, Kadaga tells government. The Monitor. 3 July 2017

> in her illness. In March 2019 Kadaga would have the unenviable opportunity to test out the efficiency of the approval procedures for foreign medical travel. She was briefly admitted to Nakasero Hospital, a high-end private hospital in Kampala, before being med-evacuated to Nairobi for further hospitalization.

***

Namubiru was just returning from leave. She had lost the bet on the new opening date for the renovated New Mulago Hospital. Nobody seemed to know what the new date was, but the beginning of June had come and gone. The only news was the national budget. Sometimes the doctors discussed it, but lately most were ignoring it altogether. References to increased pay for doctors were usually rosier than the reality. Namubiru had read the speech with the usual resigned indifference, but one short section had stayed with her all morning: '*53% of children under five years are malnourished and hence anemic, and 29% of them are stunted or wasted. Many women of reproductive age are also malnourished, with 32% of them being anemic.*'[74] She had stayed clear of politics all these years, but she was now admitting to herself that Uganda seemed to be in crisis. She was still thinking about this when she walked into the department. As though fate was stalking her thoughts, the first people she ran into were Namisi and Agaba. She quickly realized that they were talking about the budget. She surprised the two men by chipping in. "I don't know where you two stand on this but I think for the first time – or maybe I missed it all these years – the government is being frank about the gravity of the situation. If nothing else gets our attention, the levels of malnutrition are at crisis levels."

Namisi and Agaba must have been shocked that Namubiru was commenting on something bordering on the political. Namisi recovered quickly enough. "It is not right to think of this as a crisis. The country

---

[74] Budget Speech Financial Year 2019/20. Theme: Industrialization for Job creation and shared prosperity, delivered at the 4th session of the 10th Parliament of Uganda by Hon. Matia Kasaija (MP) Minister of Finance, Planning and Economic Development. 13 June 2019

did not crash this year, and it will not bounce back in a hurry. It has been failing for a long time. It has finally exhausted its reserve capacity. When more than half of a country's future is malnourished, we know that country is staring failure in the face. Where are our thinkers going to come from? Who will be our teachers? Engineers? Police Officers? Who will pay taxes? Sure, there will still be the odd star, the exceptional genius. But countries are not developed by the exceptions. A house needs hundreds of thousands of good regular bricks to stand, not just the strong cornerstones. In Uganda the regular bricks are prone to crumbling. This is failure. The middle income status is a pipe dream.'

***

Karungi stood outside the Heart Institute pondering the easiest way to her car, all the way down by the Students' canteen at the medical school. She had parked there planning to be gone for an hour at most. She had not intended to spend the public holiday at the hospital. Now it was several hours, and she hoped the car would be intact. There had been many instances of vehicles being stripped of lights and mirrors in the medical school and hospital parking. The shortest route was also the roughest, but she decided to take chances with it. The path came down by the old Department of Medical Illustration, leaving the Sickle Cell Clinic to the right. It was hard to know where the original paved road had been. The entire path was one pothole after another. As she passed by the old Ward 16 she saw a big sign at the entrance announcing that the ward was now called Jellife Ward, no doubt after Dr. J.B. Jellife, one of the founding fathers of pediatrics in Mulago Hospital. The building had been given a fresh coat of paint, so it stood in stark contrast to the ancient and rusty-looking roofs and windows. A rickety looking kiosk stood a short distance away from the ward entrance, with an equally rickety board announcing that one could buy airtime and get mobile money services there. Karungi picked her way gingerly along the uneven path with its loose gravel. The space between the old animal house-turned-offices and the Department of Anatomy building was dark but easy enough to maneuver. The narrow aperture was more a hole in the wall than a proper gate, and it had been the same way for decades. Stepping through this small gate, she now faced the School of Biomedical Sciences, and had the old PG room to her right. She had not walked this way at such an hour for years. She noticed that the light was on. She was going to head straight to her car, which she could see from this point, but on impulse she decided to go and see who was in the PG room at this hour on a public holiday.

The door was ajar. Karungi pushed it wider open and looked inside. No one in sight. She was struck by how much the room had changed. The old sofa in the corner was gone. The side tables were covered with Formica. There was far better lighting than she remembered. The chairs were newer. Only one thing looked exactly the way she remembered it some 25 years previously. The board. Francis' board. She walked over towards it, aware that she was now trespassing. There was a short line of writing in the top right corner of the board. '*Martyrs' day. Heroes' day. … when is the day of the patient?*' A laptop was on in the corner where Ntege used to sit, and the screen saver was playing a random pattern with colored pipes. She could hear the sound of a flushing toilet somewhere in the building. There was a piece of chalk by the board. Following some invisible hand that propelled her on, she picked the chalk and started to write on the board.

All ye occupants of PG room. Past, present and future. Our mission is singular. To care for the well, the sick, and the dying. With haste, respect, and in dignity.

She slipped out without looking back to see if she had been spotted by whoever was coming out of the bathroom. As she turned the corner she saw a guard at the corner of the Physiology lab. For some reason she remembered the incident all those years ago when a guard had been called to PG room because a hen in the room had caused the doctors to scream for help. How things had changed. And then again, how things had stayed the same.

The physicians are the natural attorneys of the poor. Rudolf Karl Ludwig Virchow, nineteenth-century German physician (1821-1902).

Ambulances get ready to transport supplies and
patients from Kampala, early 1930s.

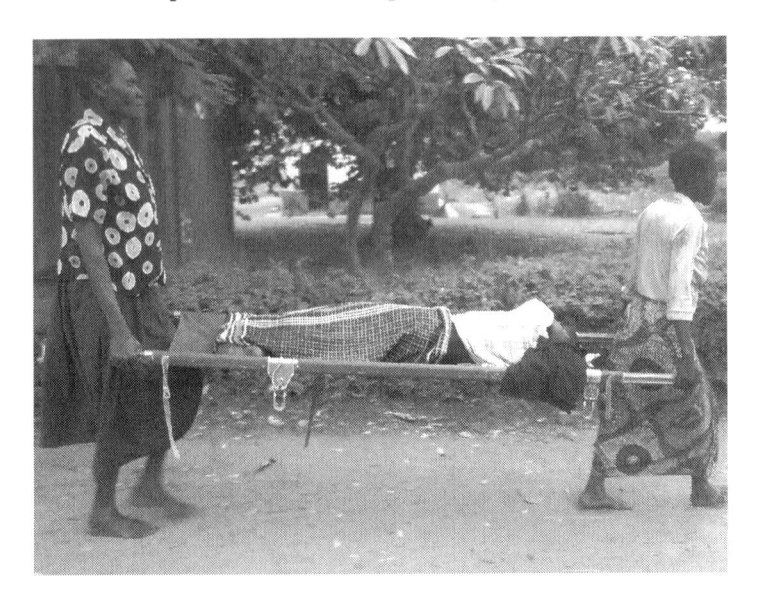

Women carry a sick relative on a stretcher to Maracha Hospital, 2013

MAKERERE UNIVERSITY ANTHEM (ABRIDGED)

'Makerere, Makerere, We build for the future, The Great Makerere

Do not forget,
Through all the years
Those who have gone through the gates of Makerere

Those who here be, Seek ye the truth
Build for the future, The great Makerere
Those here have been, Those here will be
Build for the future,
The Great Makerere

Printed in Great Britain
by Amazon